D0003274

EPISODE V
THE EMPIRE STRIKES BACK

BASED ON A STORY BY
GEORGE LUCAS

SCREENPLAY BY
LEIGH BRACKETT AND LAWRENCE KASDAN

DARK HORSE BOOKS®

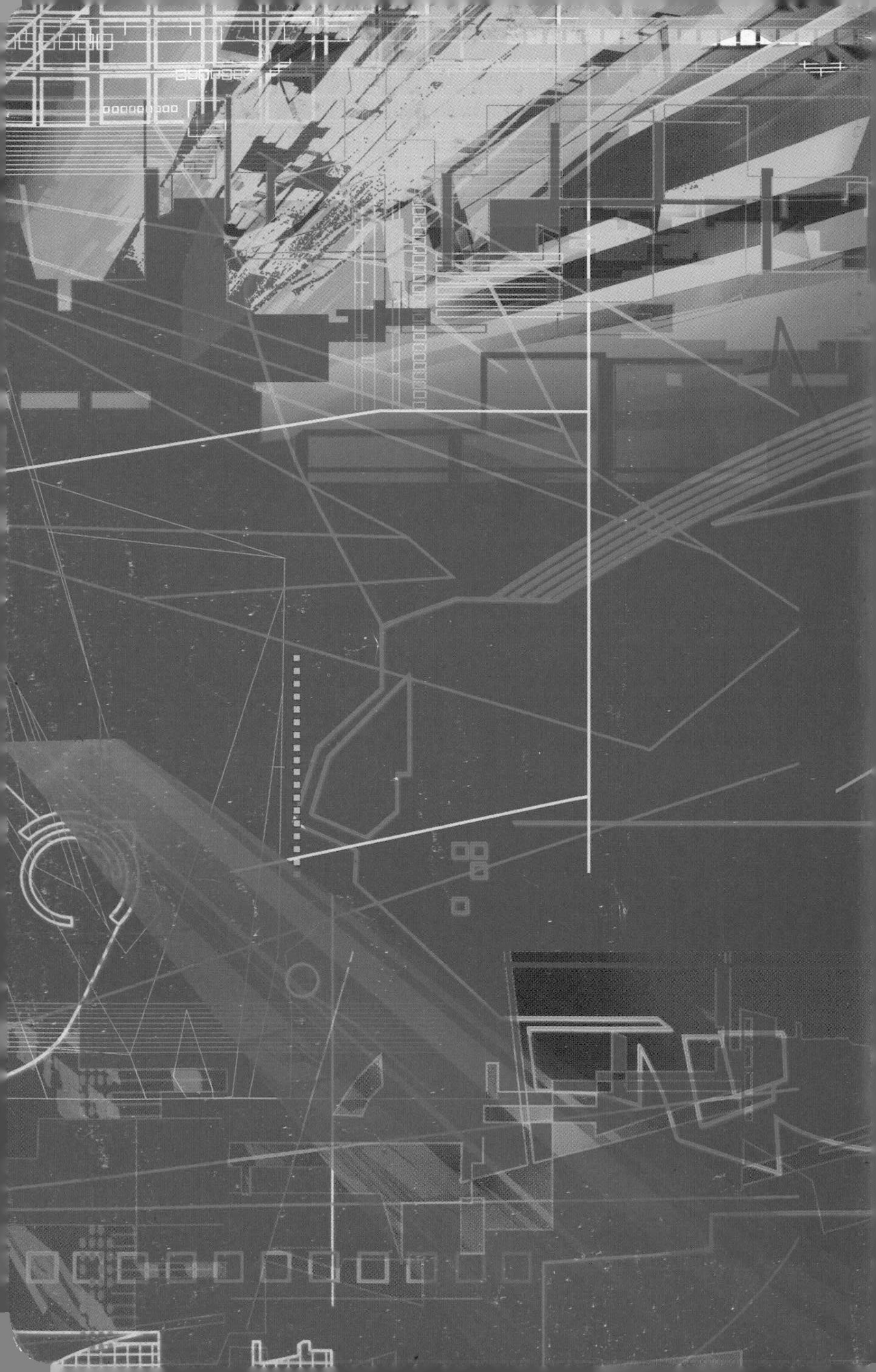

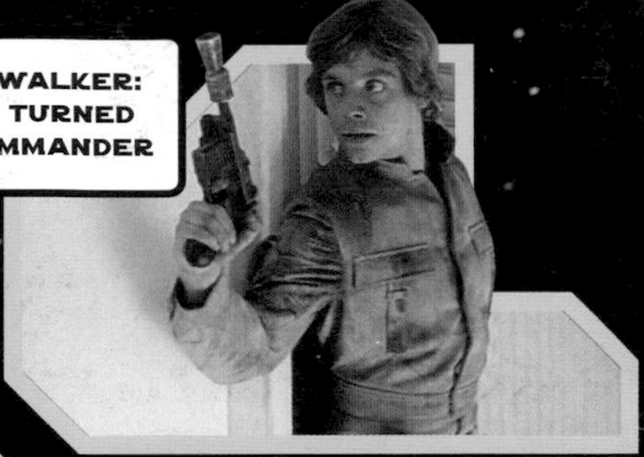

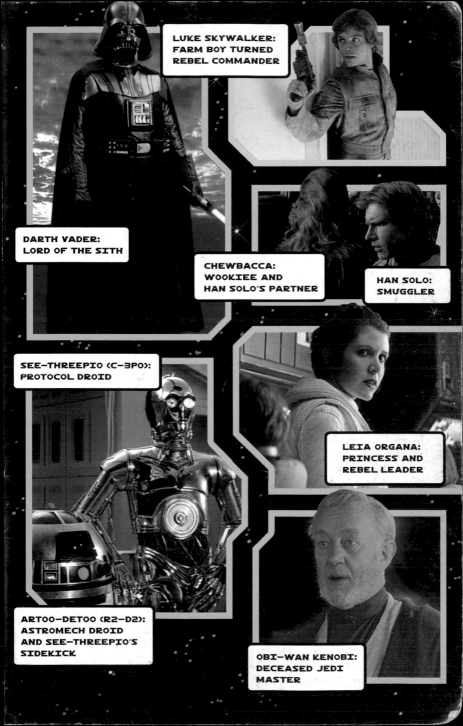

LUKE SKYWALKER:
FARM BOY TURNED
REBEL COMMANDER

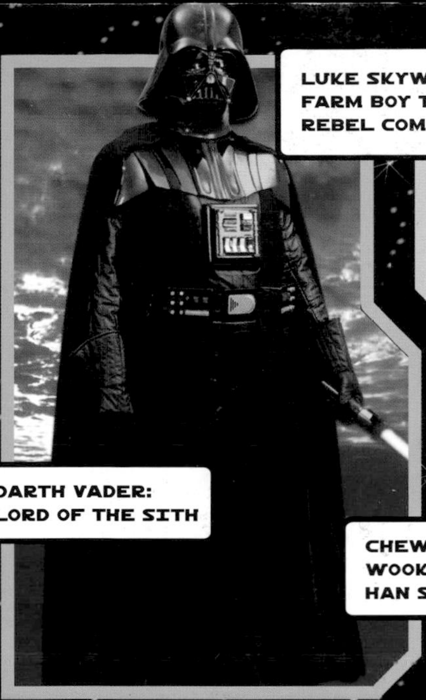

DARTH VADER:
LORD OF THE SITH

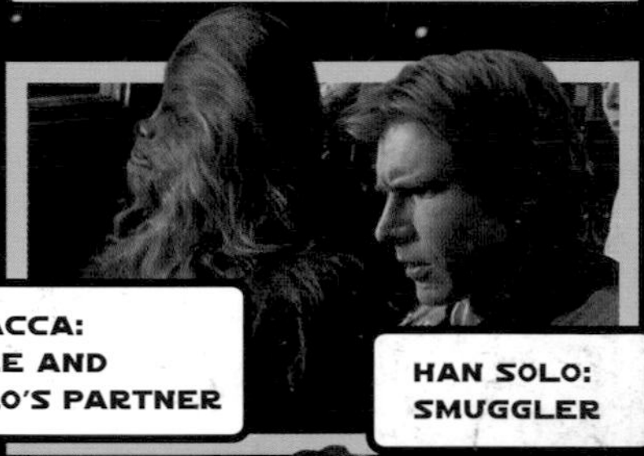

CHEWBACCA:
WOOKIEE AND
HAN SOLO'S PARTNER

HAN SOLO:
SMUGGLER

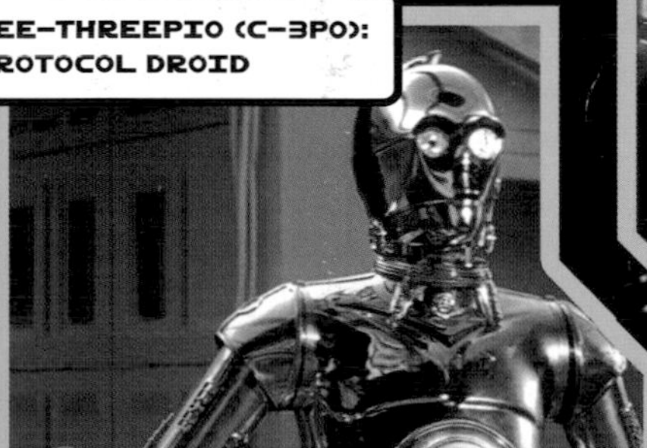

SEE-THREEPIO (C-3PO):
PROTOCOL DROID

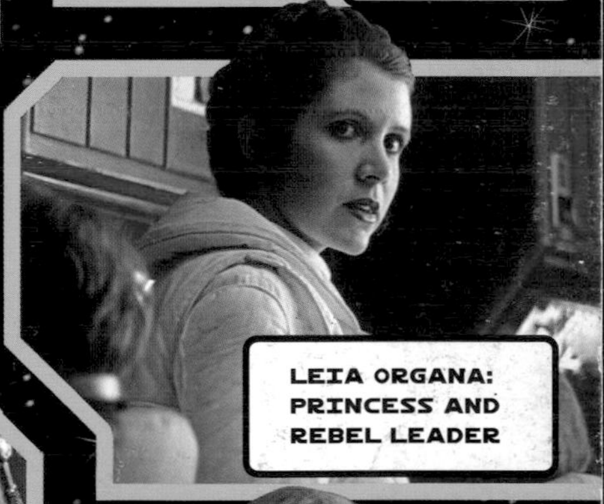

LEIA ORGANA:
PRINCESS AND
REBEL LEADER

ARTOO-DETOO (R2-D2):
ASTROMECH DROID
AND SEE-THREEPIO'S
SIDEKICK

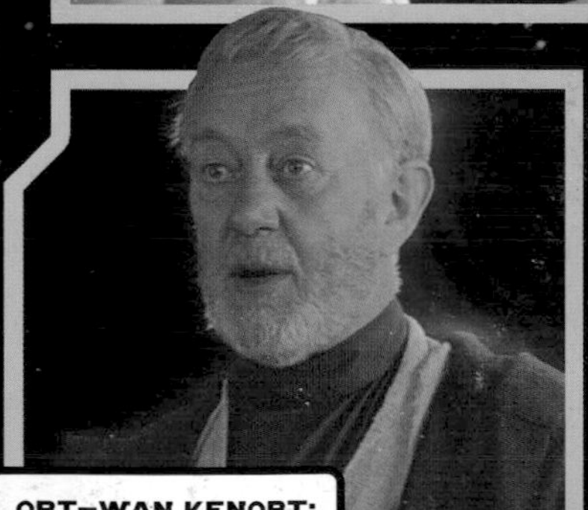

OBI-WAN KENOBI:
DECEASED JEDI
MASTER

A long time ago in a galaxy far, far away....

It is a dark time for the Rebellion. Although the Death Star has been destroyed, Imperial troops have driven the Rebel forces from their hidden base and pursued them across the galaxy.

Evading the dreaded Imperial Starfleet, a group of freedom fighters led by Luke Skywalker has established a new secret base on the remote ice world of Hoth.

The evil lord Darth Vader, obsessed with finding young Skywalker, has dispatched thousands of remote probes into the far reaches of space....

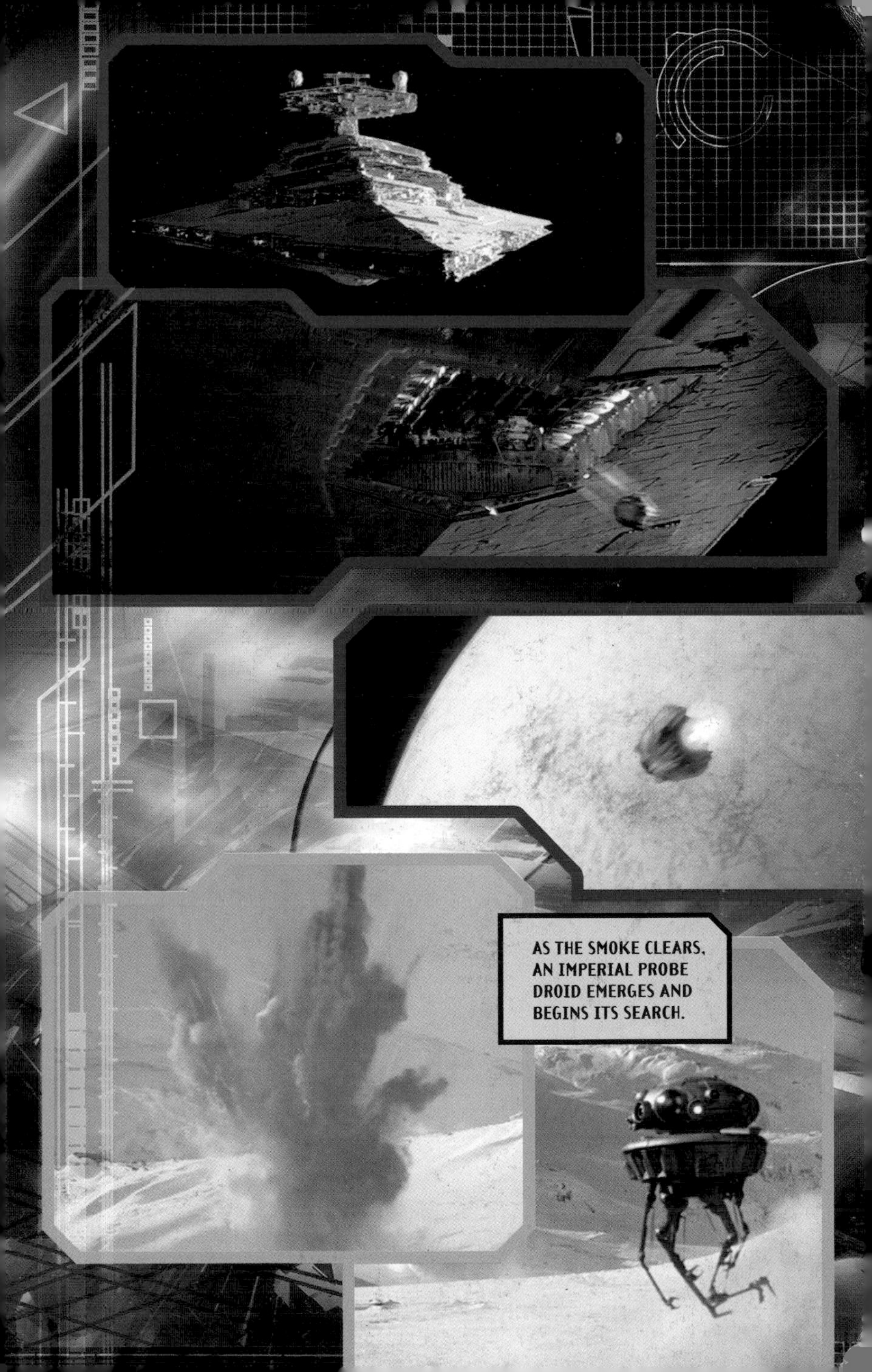
AS THE SMOKE CLEARS, AN IMPERIAL PROBE DROID EMERGES AND BEGINS ITS SEARCH.

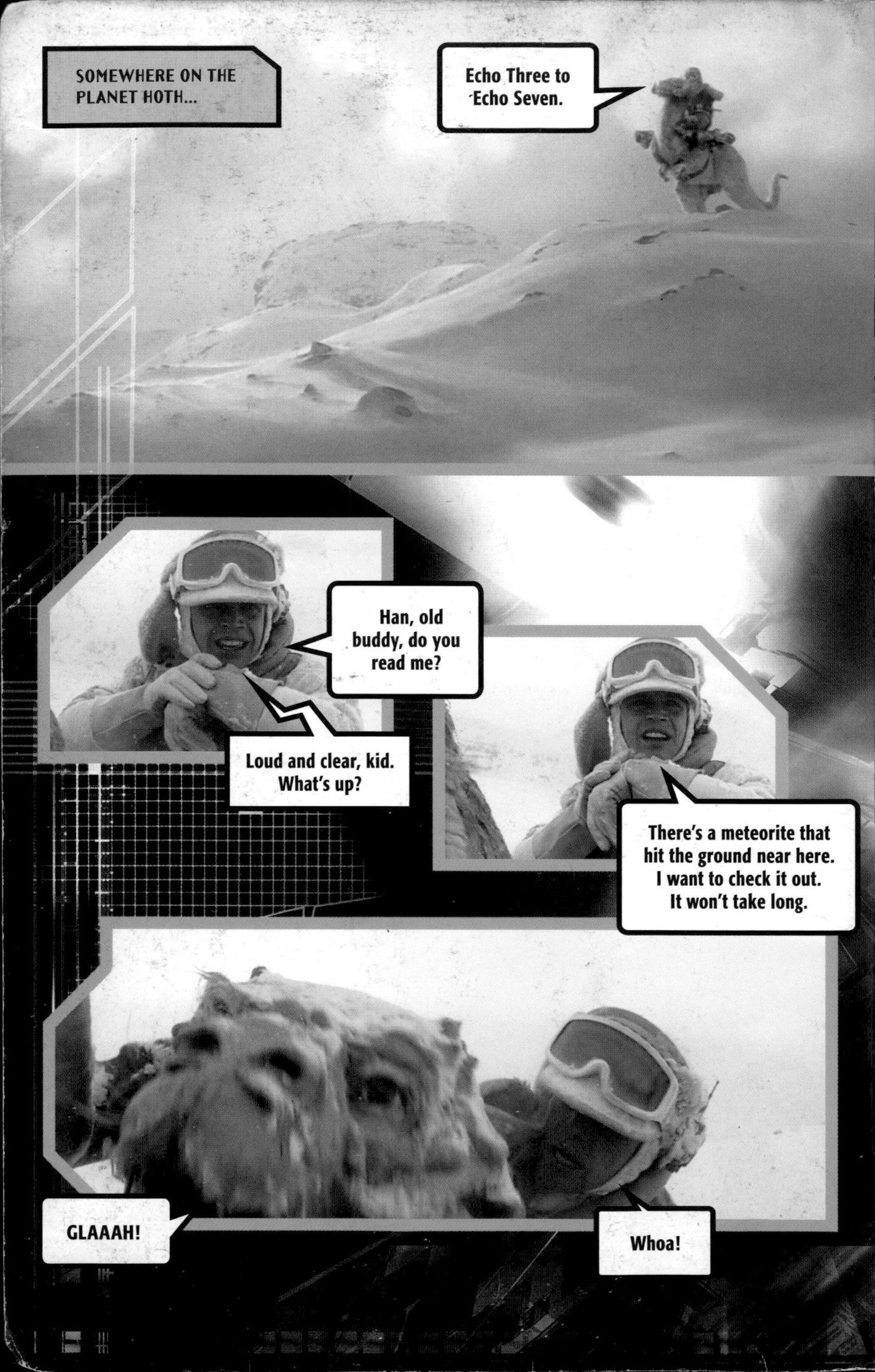
SOMEWHERE ON THE PLANET HOTH...
Echo Three to Echo Seven.
Han, old buddy, do you read me?
Loud and clear, kid. What's up?
There's a meteorite that hit the ground near here. I want to check it out. It won't take long.
GLAAAH!
Whoa!

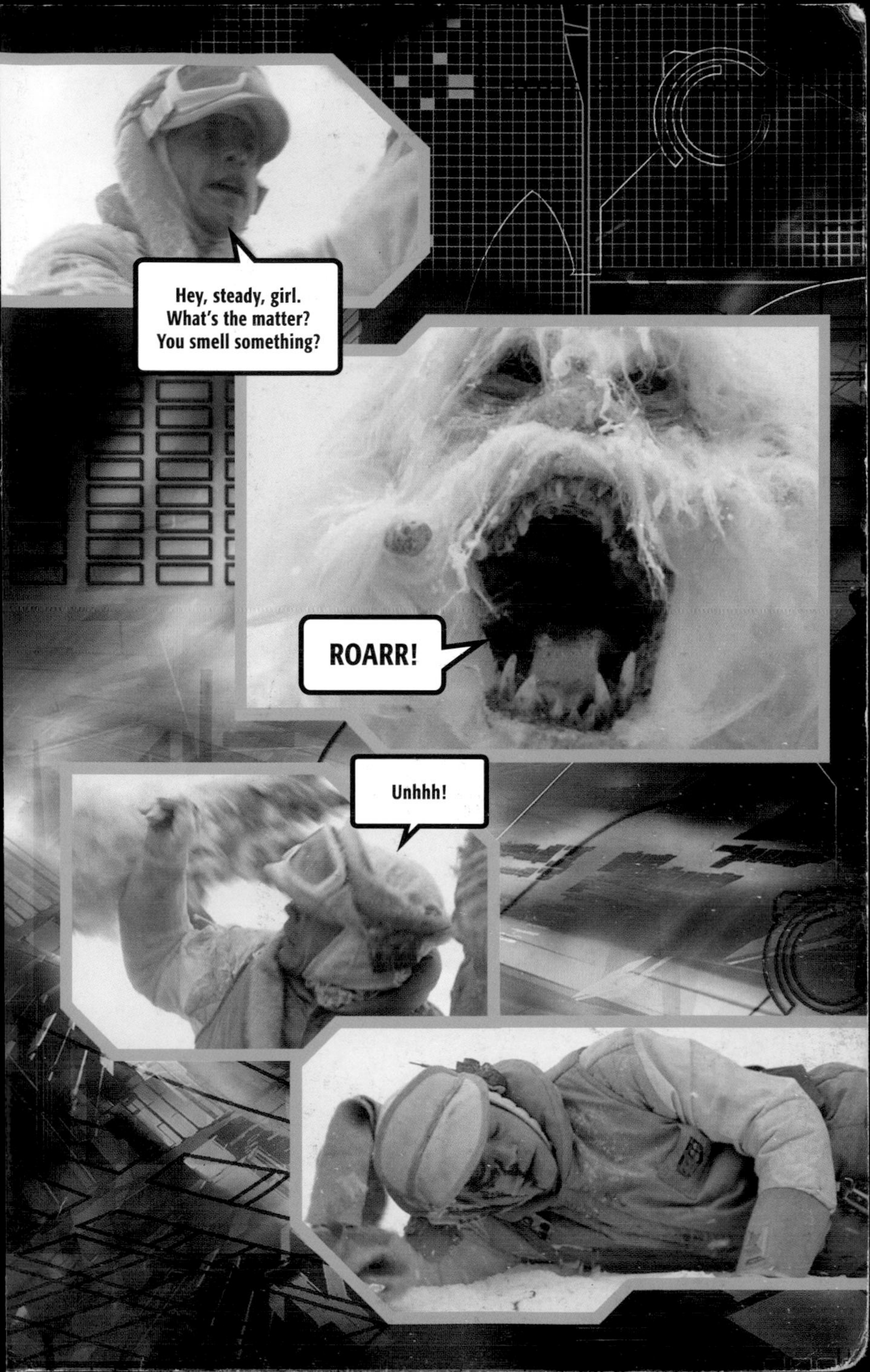
Hey, steady, girl.
What's the matter?
You smell something?
ROARR!
Unhhh!

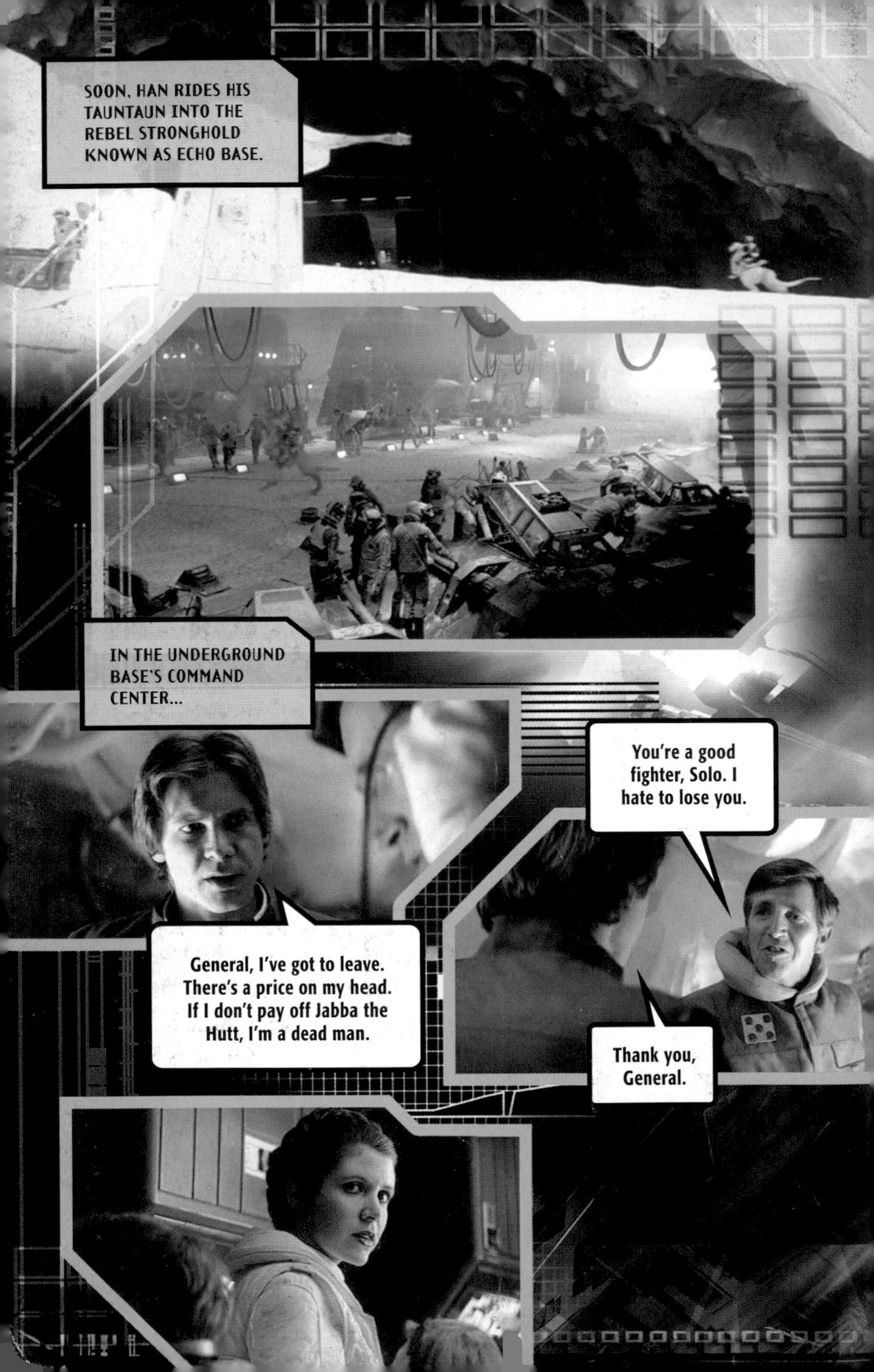
SOON, HAN RIDES HIS TAUNTAUN INTO THE REBEL STRONGHOLD KNOWN AS ECHO BASE.
IN THE UNDERGROUND BASE'S COMMAND CENTER...
General, I've got to leave. There's a price on my head. If I don't pay off Jabba the Hutt, I'm a dead man.
You're a good fighter, Solo. I hate to lose you.
Thank you, General.

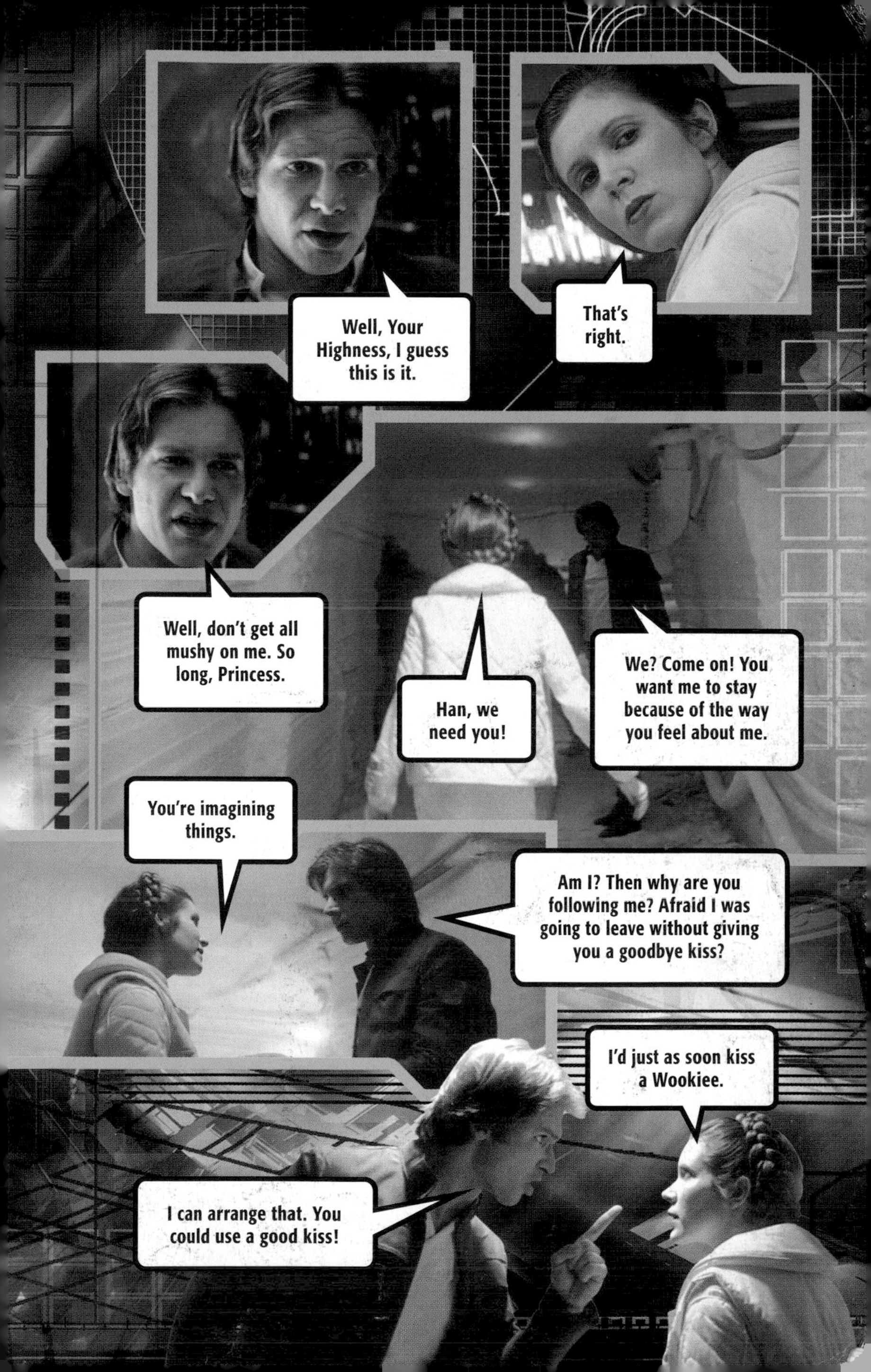
Well, Your Highness, I guess this is it.
That's right.
Well, don't get all mushy on me. So long, Princess.
Han, we need you!
We? Come on! You want me to stay because of the way you feel about me.
You're imagining things.
Am I? Then why are you following me? Afraid I was going to leave without giving you a goodbye kiss?
I'd just as soon kiss a Wookiee.
I can arrange that. You could use a good kiss!

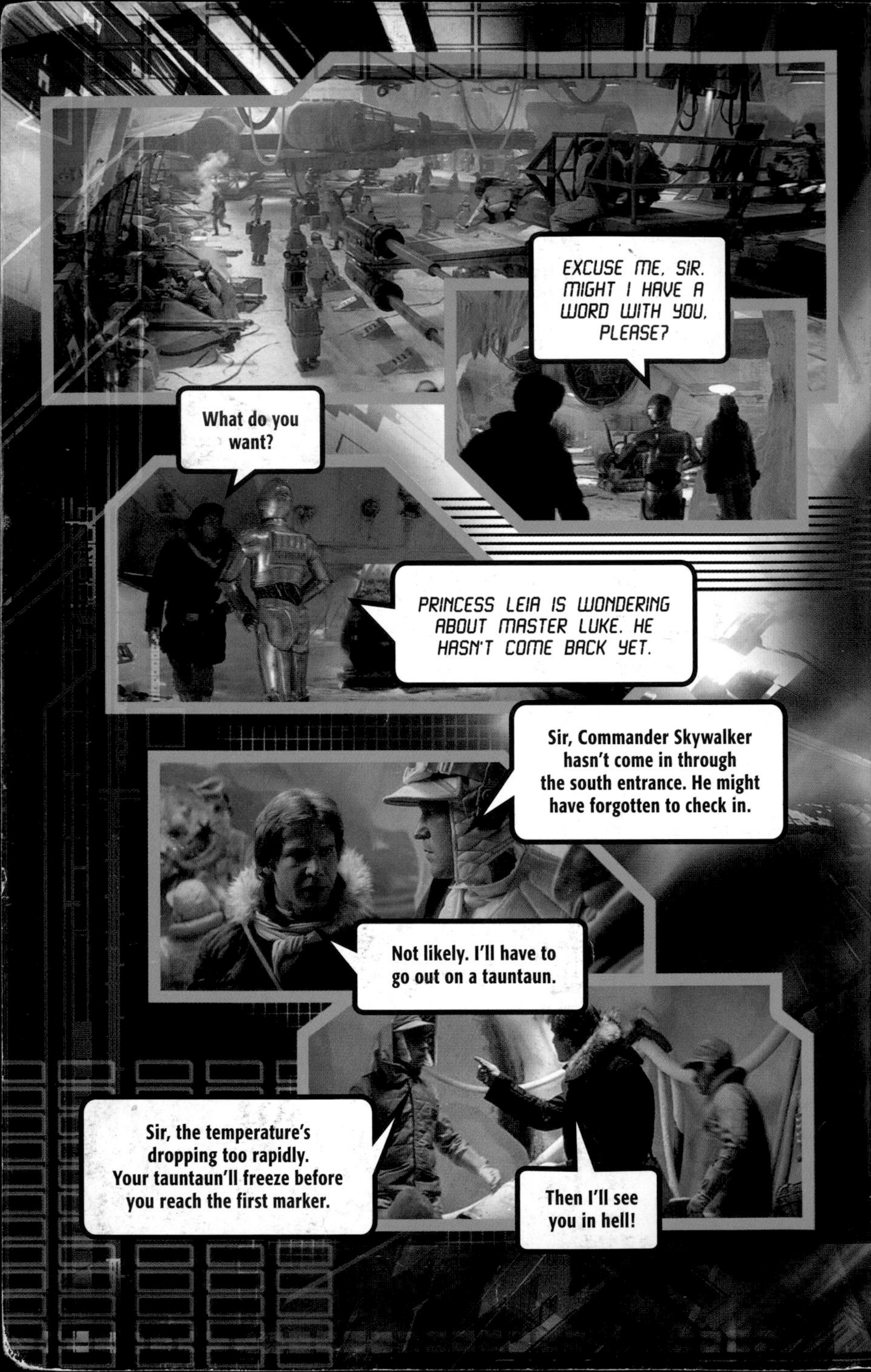
EXCUSE ME, SIR. MIGHT I HAVE A WORD WITH YOU, PLEASE?
What do you want?
PRINCESS LEIA IS WONDERING ABOUT MASTER LUKE. HE HASN'T COME BACK YET.
Sir, Commander Skywalker hasn't come in through the south entrance. He might have forgotten to check in.
Not likely. I'll have to go out on a tauntaun.
Sir, the temperature's dropping too rapidly. Your tauntaun'll freeze before you reach the first marker.
Then I'll see you in hell!

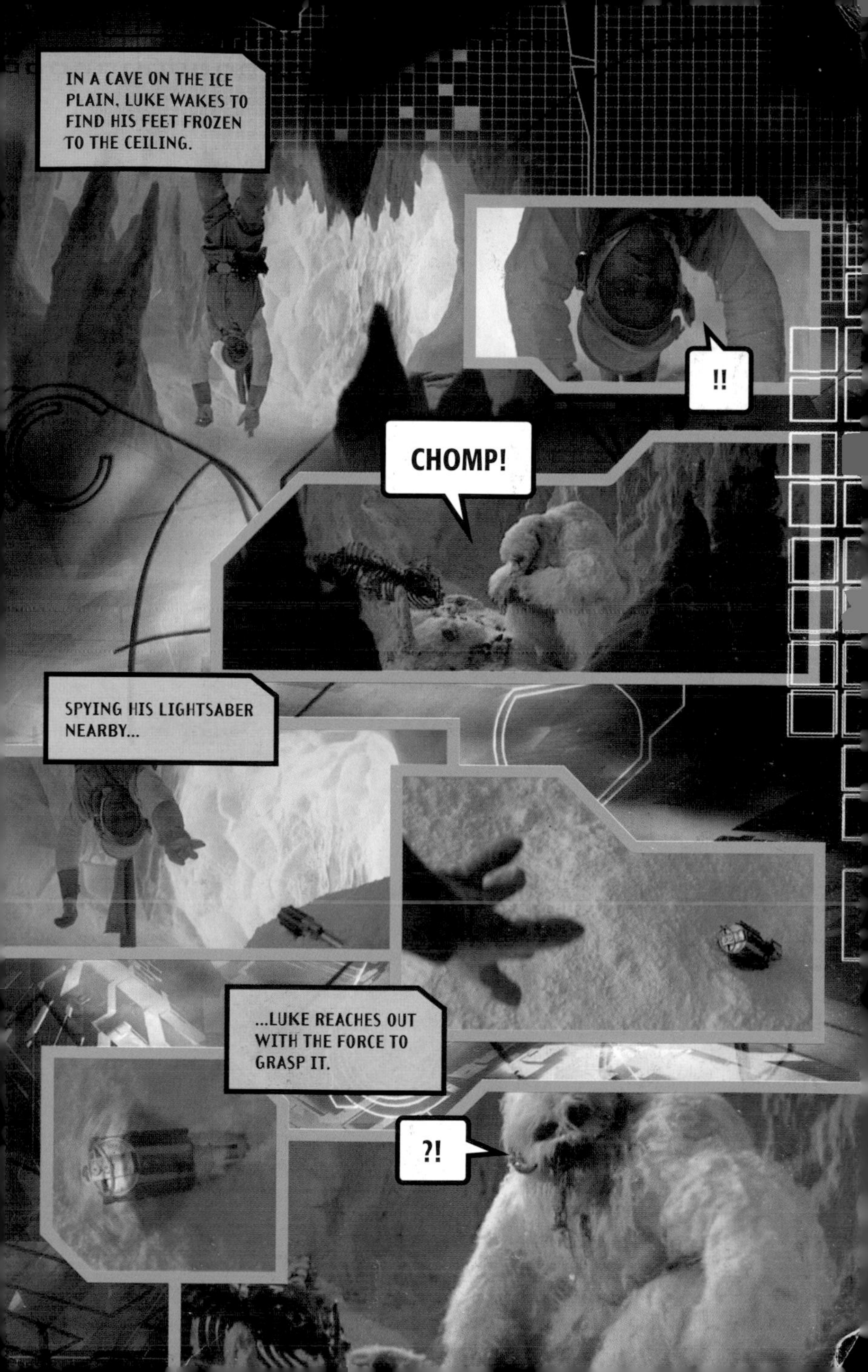
IN A CAVE ON THE ICE PLAIN, LUKE WAKES TO FIND HIS FEET FROZEN TO THE CEILING.
!!
CHOMP!
SPYING HIS LIGHTSABER NEARBY...
...LUKE REACHES OUT WITH THE FORCE TO GRASP IT.
?!

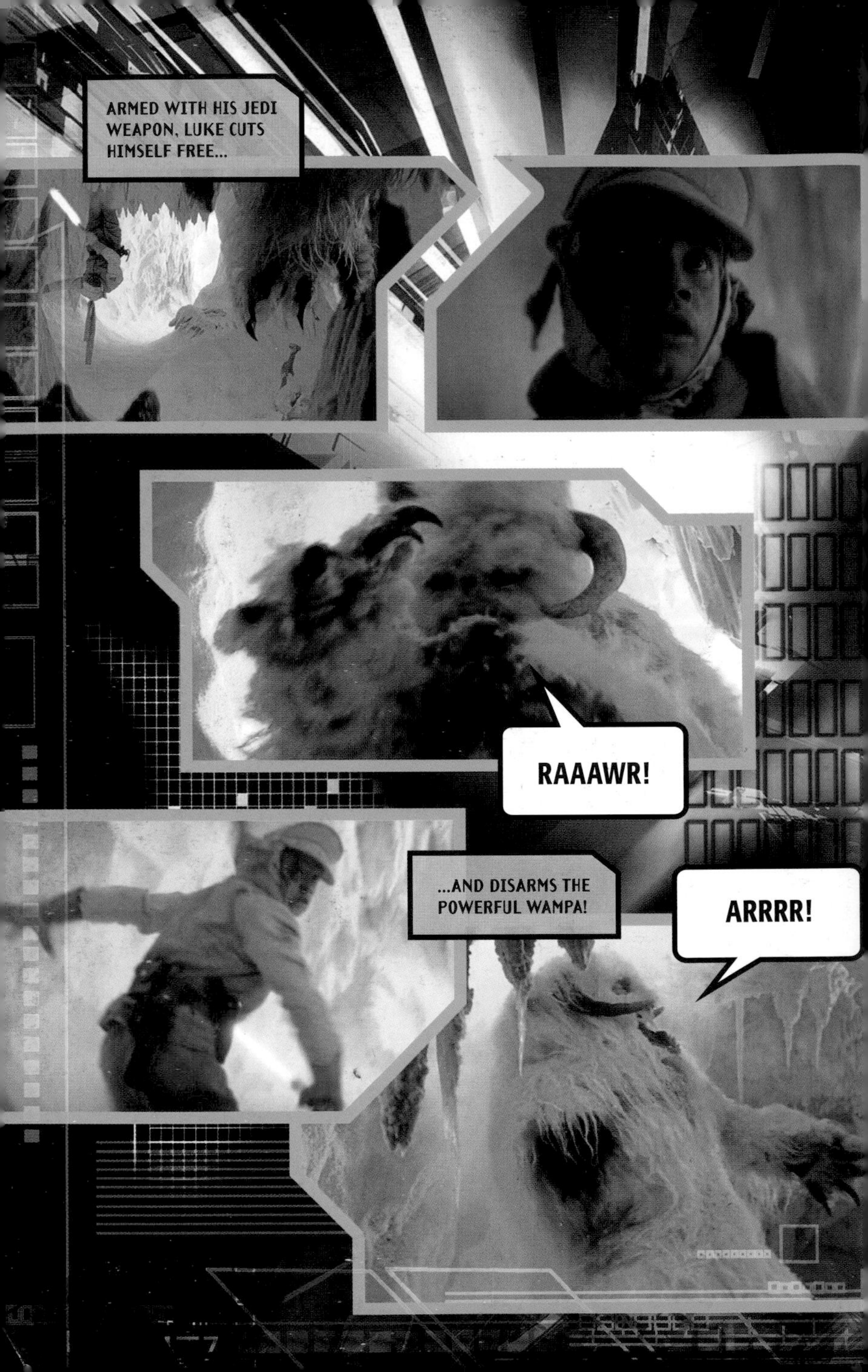
ARMED WITH HIS JEDI WEAPON, LUKE CUTS HIMSELF FREE...
RAAAWR!
...AND DISARMS THE POWERFUL WAMPA!
ARRRR!

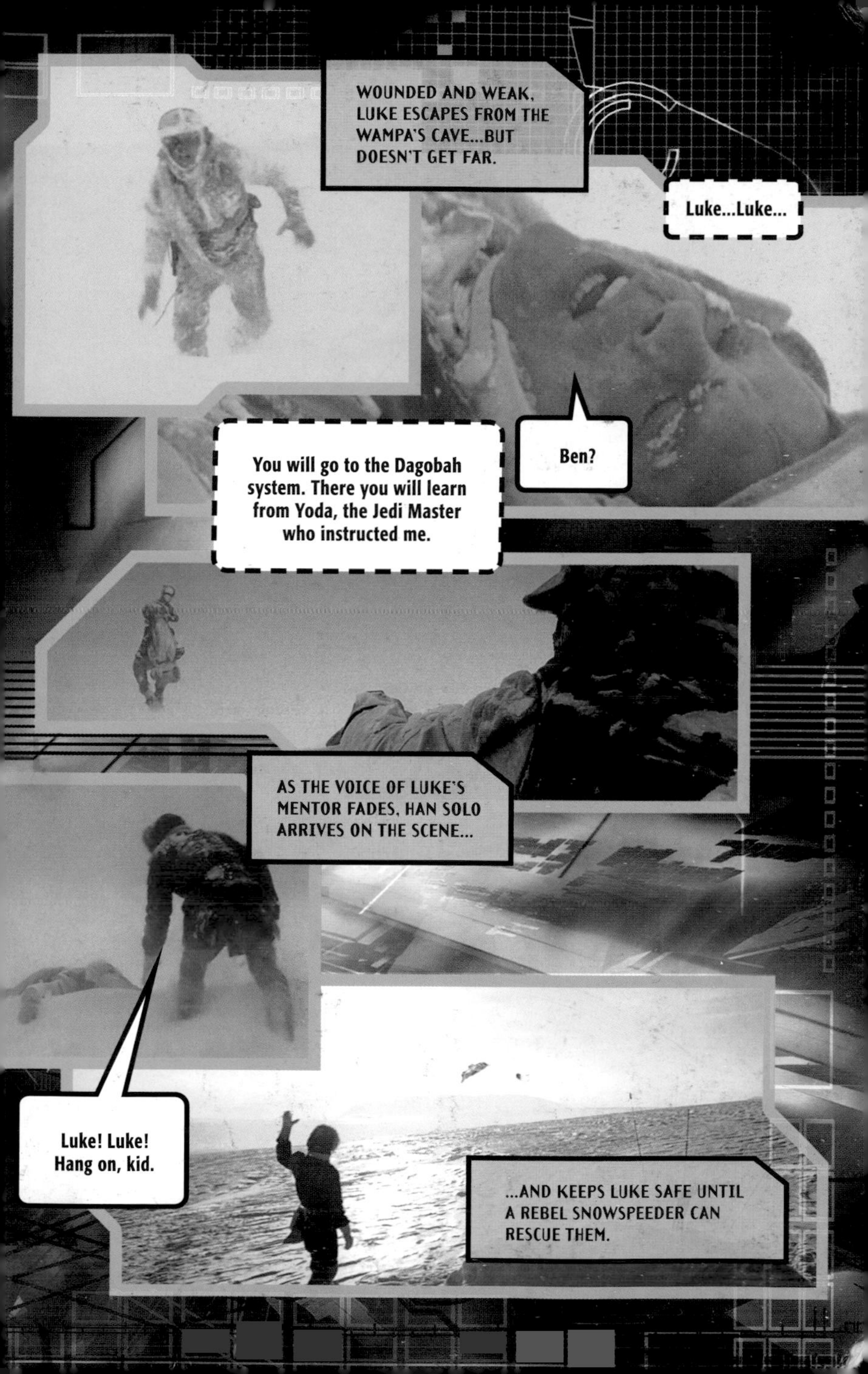
WOUNDED AND WEAK, LUKE ESCAPES FROM THE WAMPA'S CAVE...BUT DOESN'T GET FAR.
Luke...Luke...
Ben?
You will go to the Dagobah system. There you will learn from Yoda, the Jedi Master who instructed me.
AS THE VOICE OF LUKE'S MENTOR FADES, HAN SOLO ARRIVES ON THE SCENE...
Luke! Luke! Hang on, kid.
...AND KEEPS LUKE SAFE UNTIL A REBEL SNOWSPEEDER CAN RESCUE THEM.

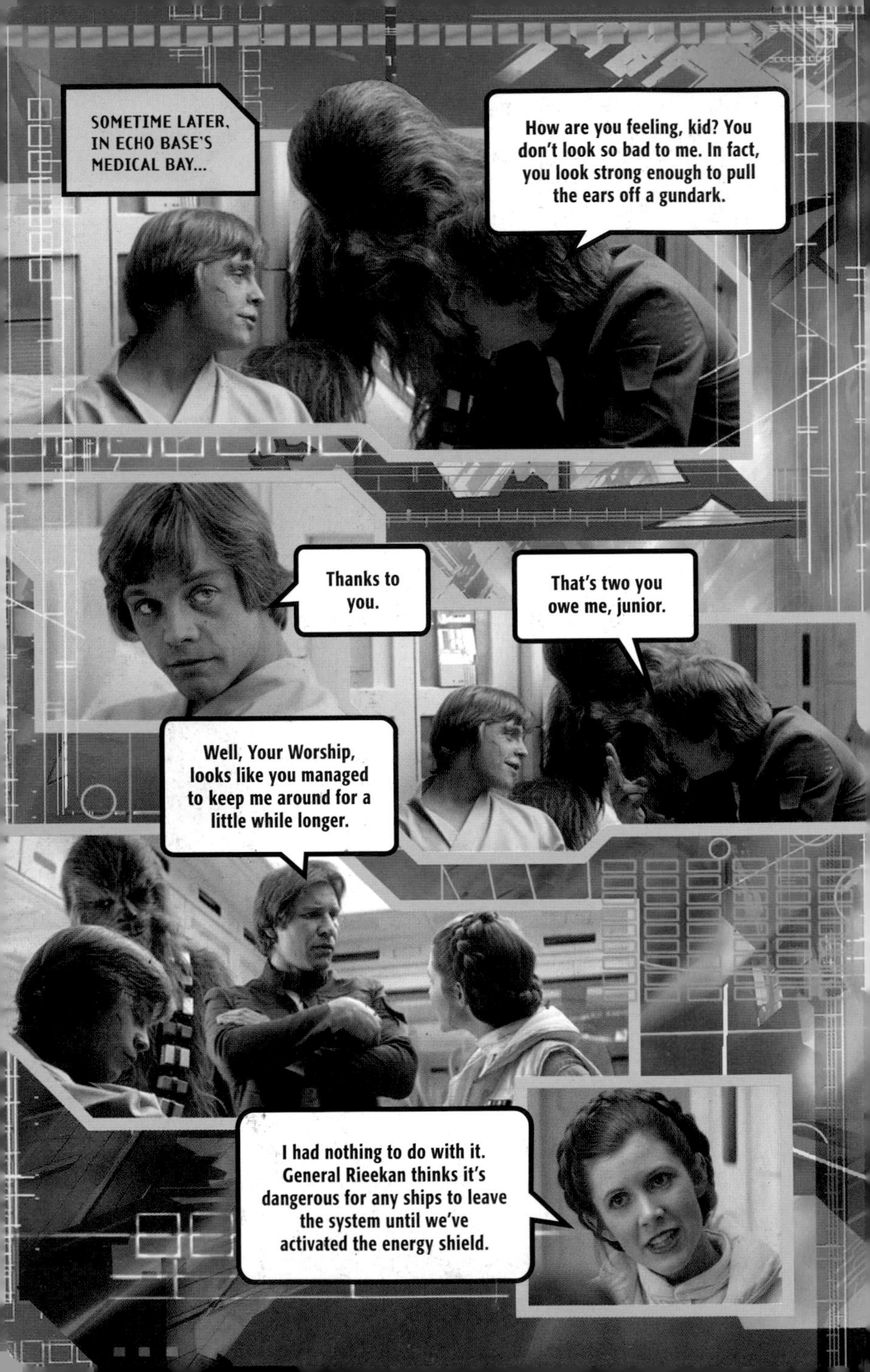
SOMETIME LATER, IN ECHO BASE'S MEDICAL BAY...
How are you feeling, kid? You don't look so bad to me. In fact, you look strong enough to pull the ears off a gundark.
Thanks to you.
That's two you owe me, junior.
Well, Your Worship, looks like you managed to keep me around for a little while longer.
I had nothing to do with it. General Rieekan thinks it's dangerous for any ships to leave the system until we've activated the energy shield.

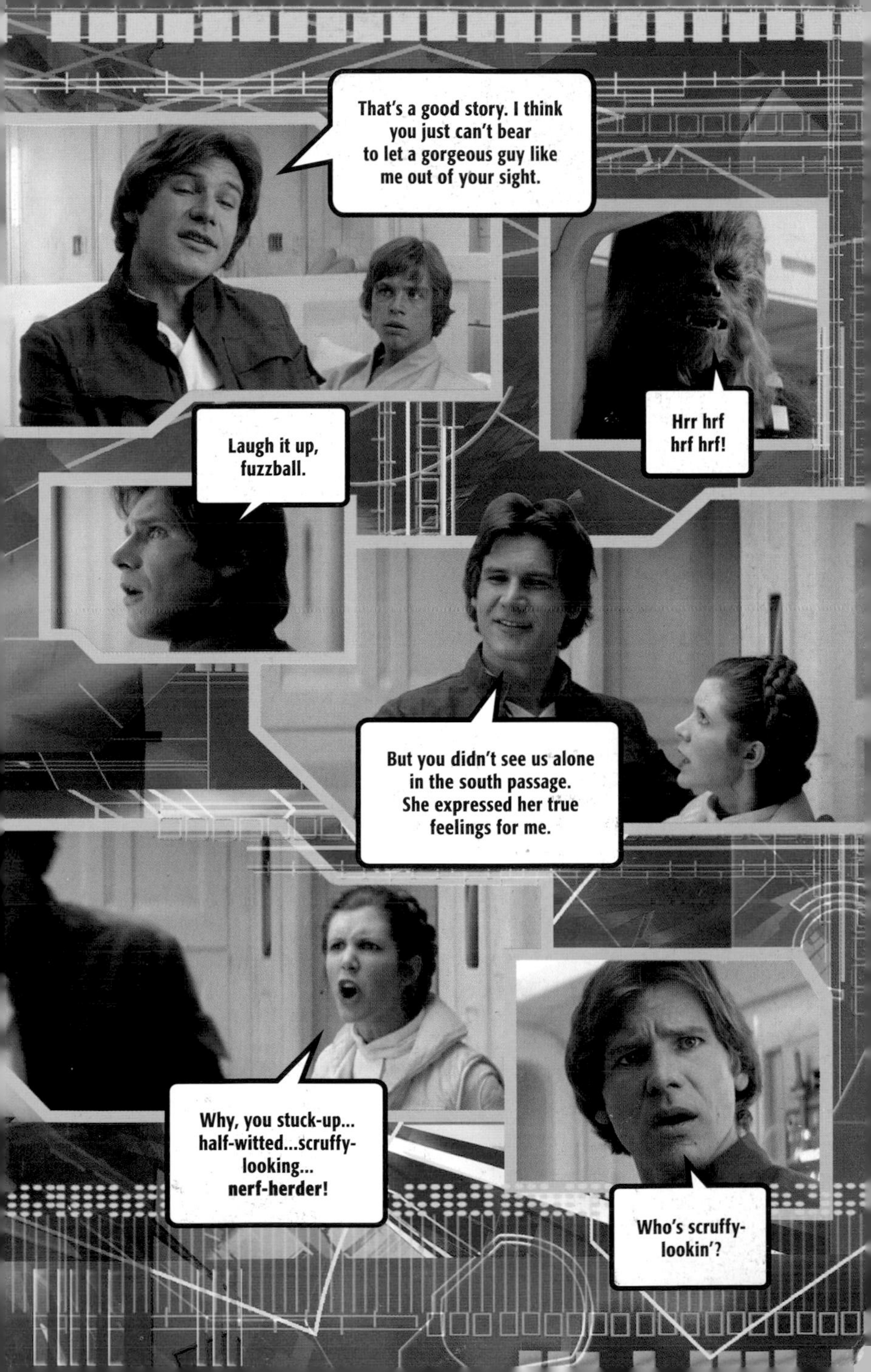
That's a good story. I think you just can't bear to let a gorgeous guy like me out of your sight.
Hrr hrf hrf hrf!
Laugh it up, fuzzball.
But you didn't see us alone in the south passage. She expressed her true feelings for me.
Why, you stuck-up... half-witted...scruffy-looking... nerf-herder!
Who's scruffy-lookin'?

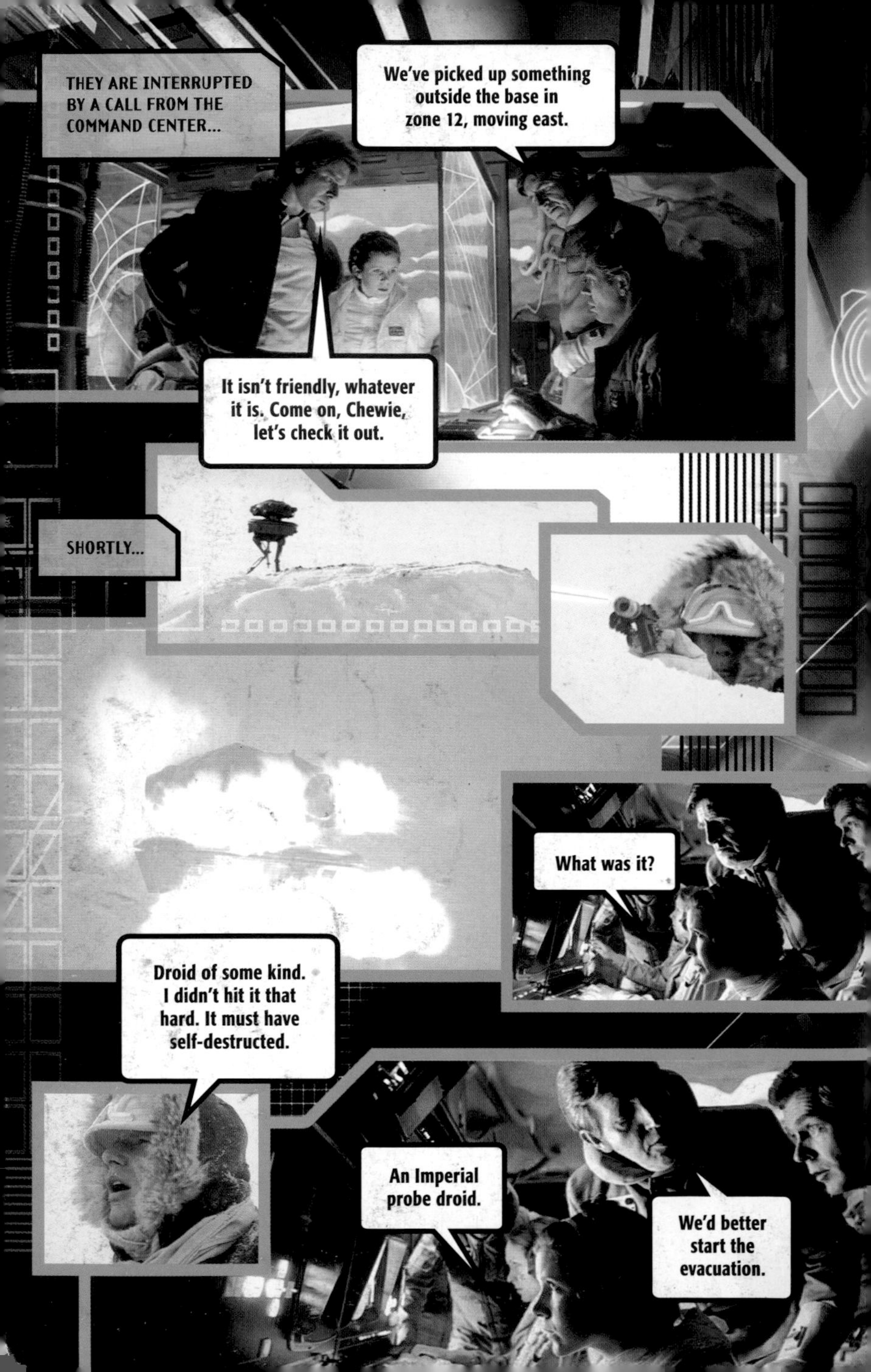
THEY ARE INTERRUPTED BY A CALL FROM THE COMMAND CENTER...
We've picked up something outside the base in zone 12, moving east.
It isn't friendly, whatever it is. Come on, Chewie, let's check it out.
SHORTLY...
What was it?
Droid of some kind. I didn't hit it that hard. It must have self-destructed.
An Imperial probe droid.
We'd better start the evacuation.

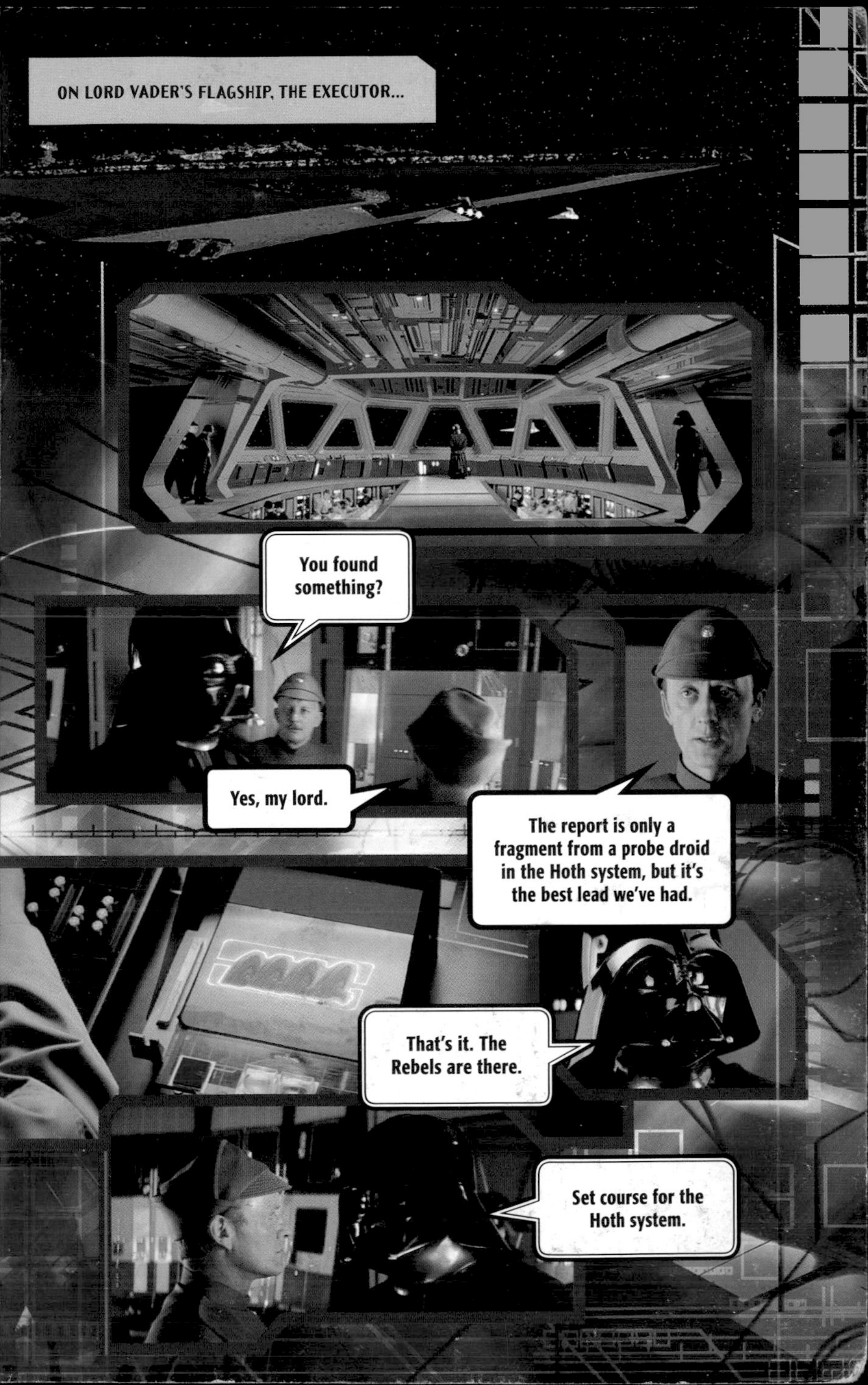
ON LORD VADER'S FLAGSHIP, THE EXECUTOR...
You found something?
Yes, my lord.
The report is only a fragment from a probe droid in the Hoth system, but it's the best lead we've had.
That's it. The Rebels are there.
Set course for the Hoth system.

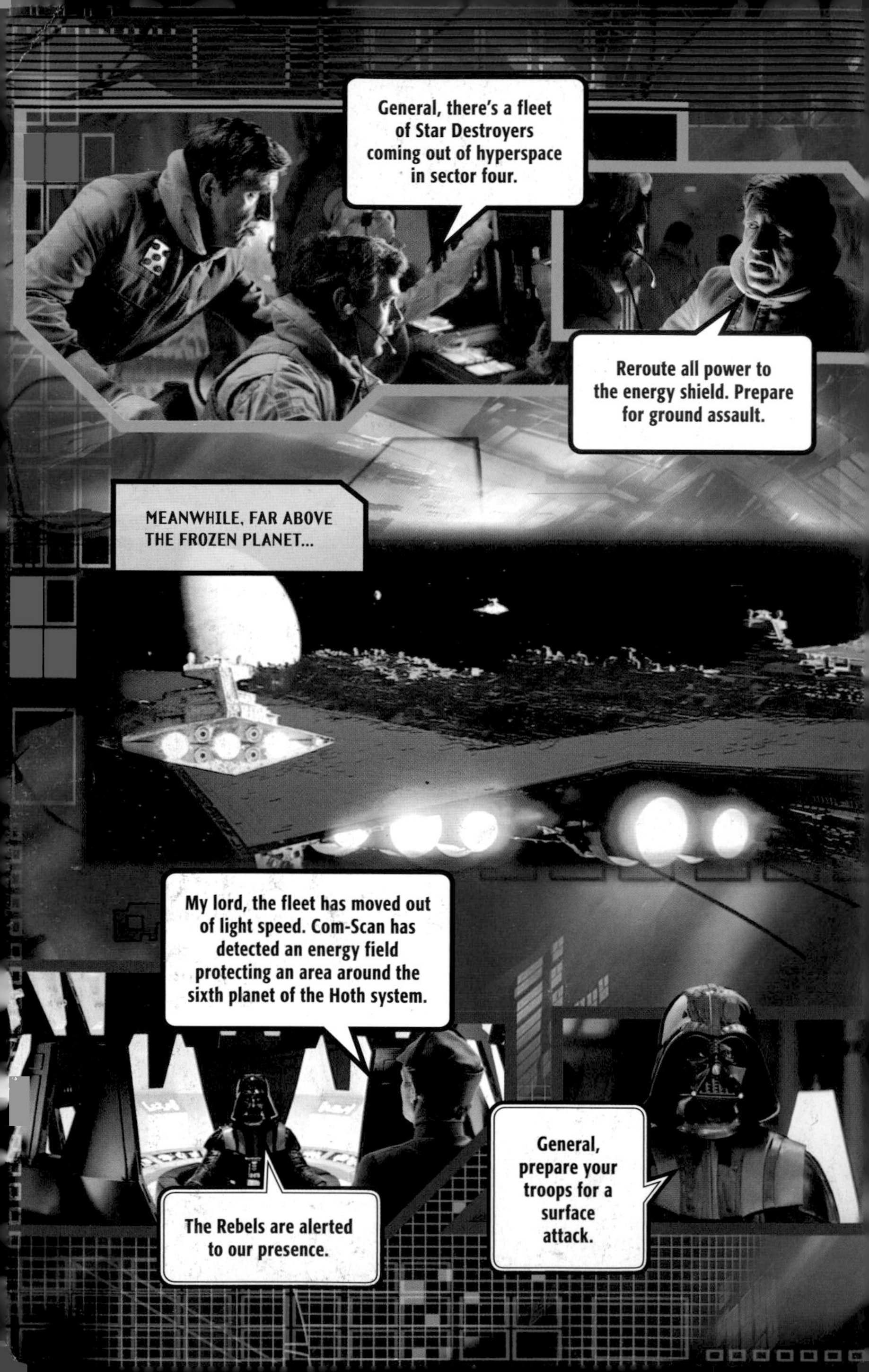
General, there's a fleet of Star Destroyers coming out of hyperspace in sector four.
Reroute all power to the energy shield. Prepare for ground assault.
MEANWHILE, FAR ABOVE THE FROZEN PLANET...
My lord, the fleet has moved out of light speed. Com-Scan has detected an energy field protecting an area around the sixth planet of the Hoth system.
The Rebels are alerted to our presence.
General, prepare your troops for a surface attack.

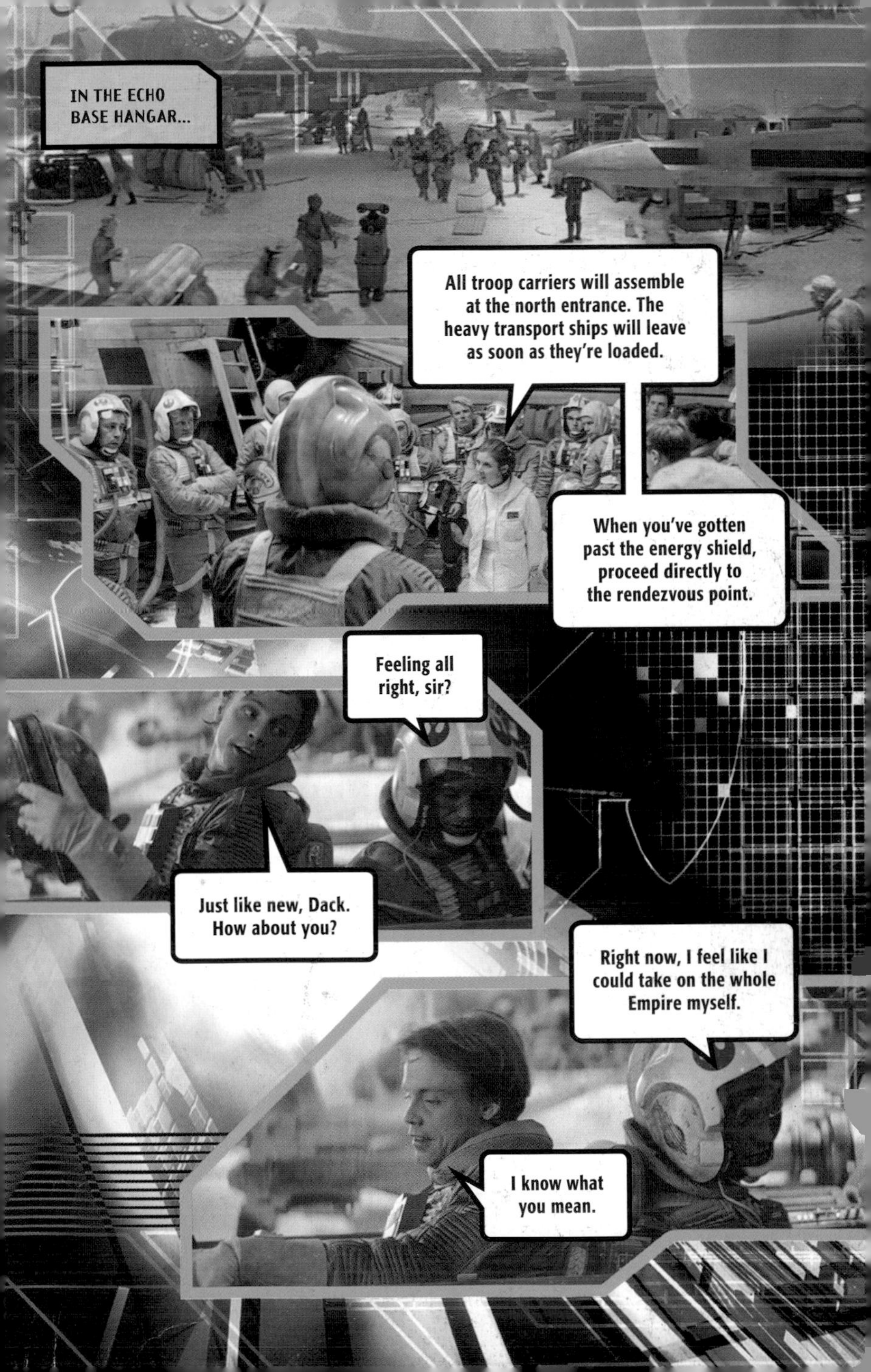

IN THE ECHO BASE HANGAR...
All troop carriers will assemble at the north entrance. The heavy transport ships will leave as soon as they're loaded.
When you've gotten past the energy shield, proceed directly to the rendezvous point.
Feeling all right, sir?
Just like new, Dack. How about you?
Right now, I feel like I could take on the whole Empire myself.
I know what you mean.

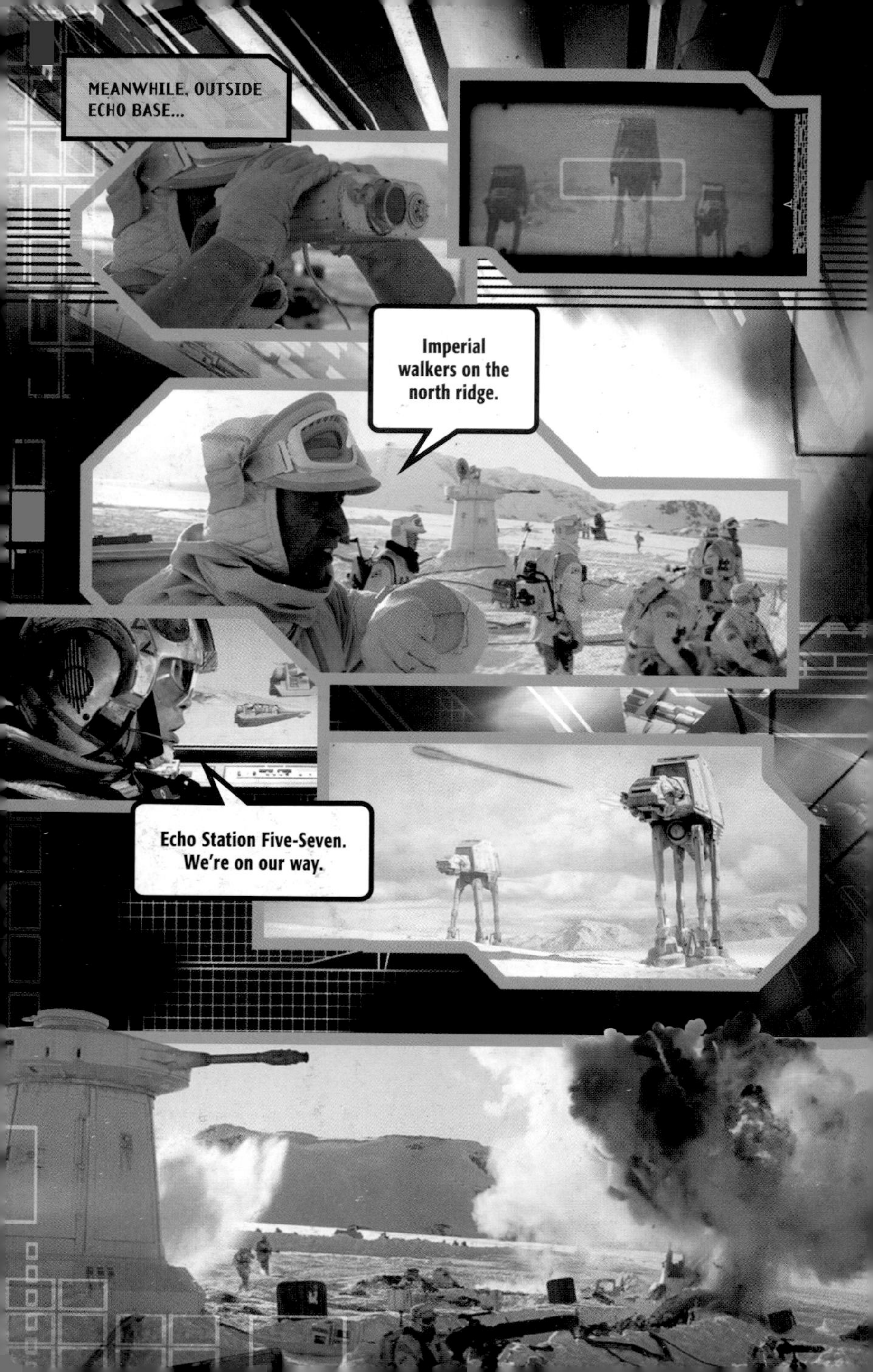
MEANWHILE, OUTSIDE ECHO BASE...
Imperial walkers on the north ridge.
Echo Station Five-Seven. We're on our way.

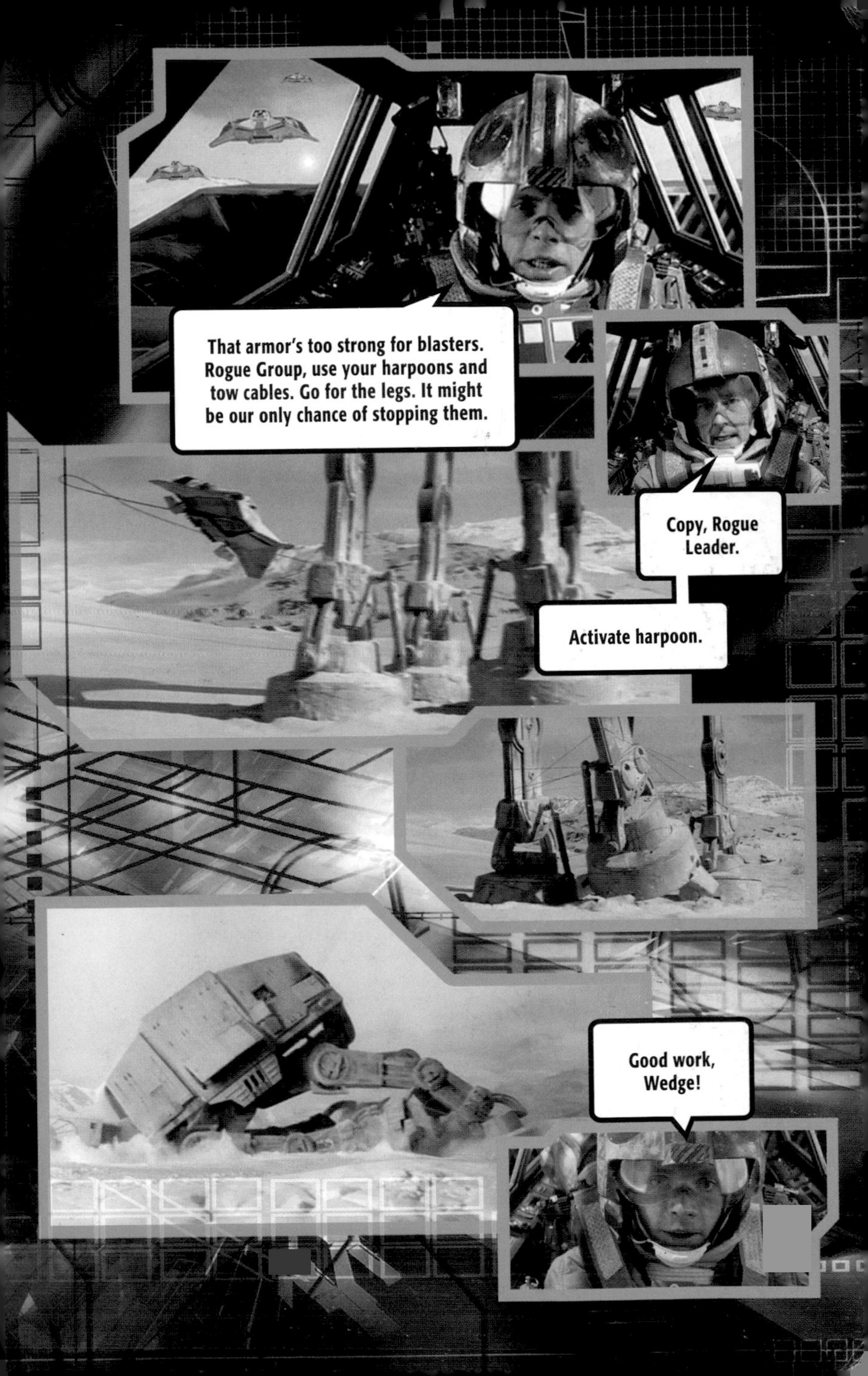
That armor's too strong for blasters. Rogue Group, use your harpoons and tow cables. Go for the legs. It might be our only chance of stopping them.
Copy, Rogue Leader.
Activate harpoon.
Good work, Wedge!

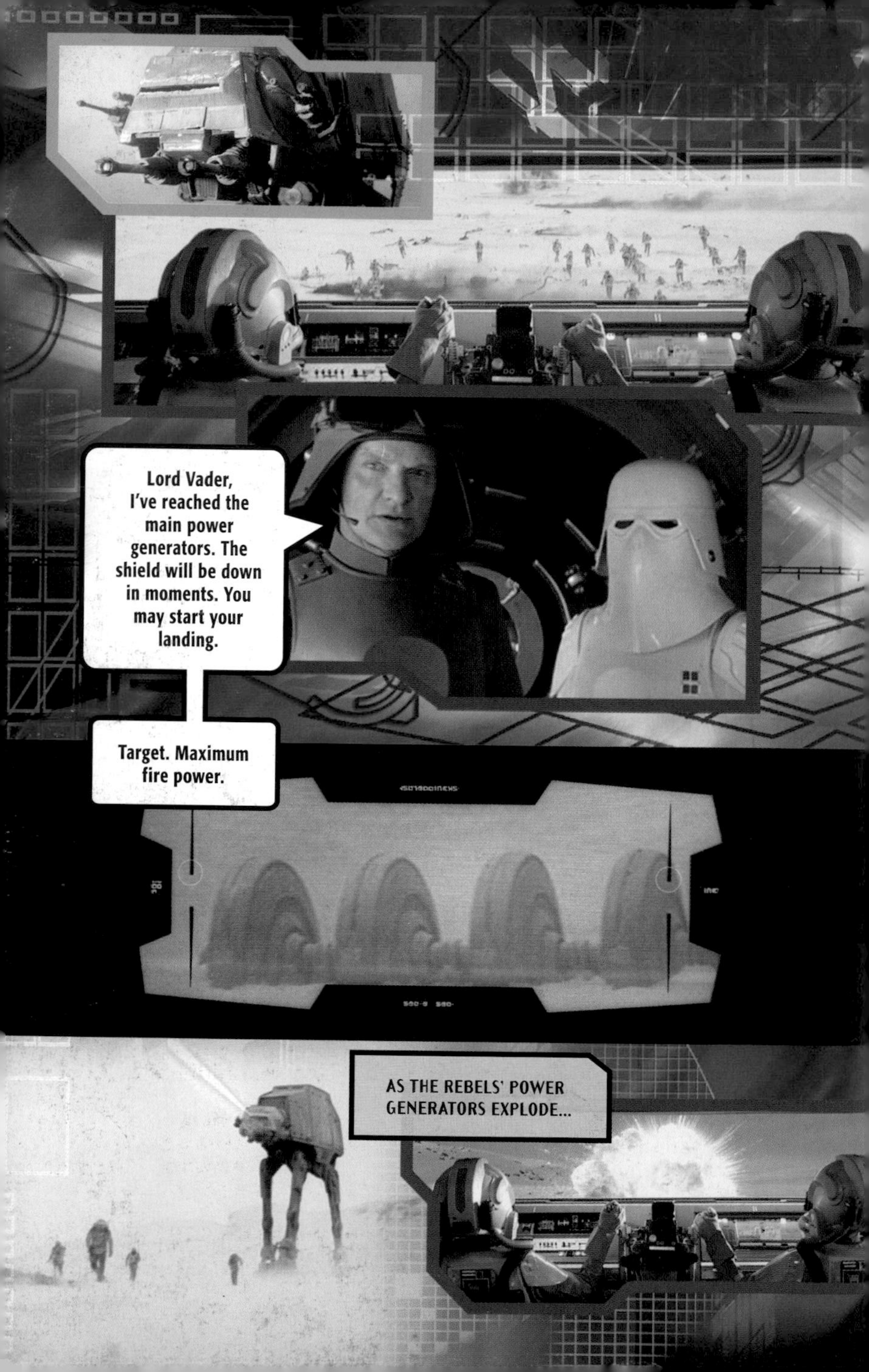
Lord Vader, I've reached the main power generators. The shield will be down in moments. You may start your landing.
Target. Maximum fire power.
AS THE REBELS' POWER GENERATORS EXPLODE...

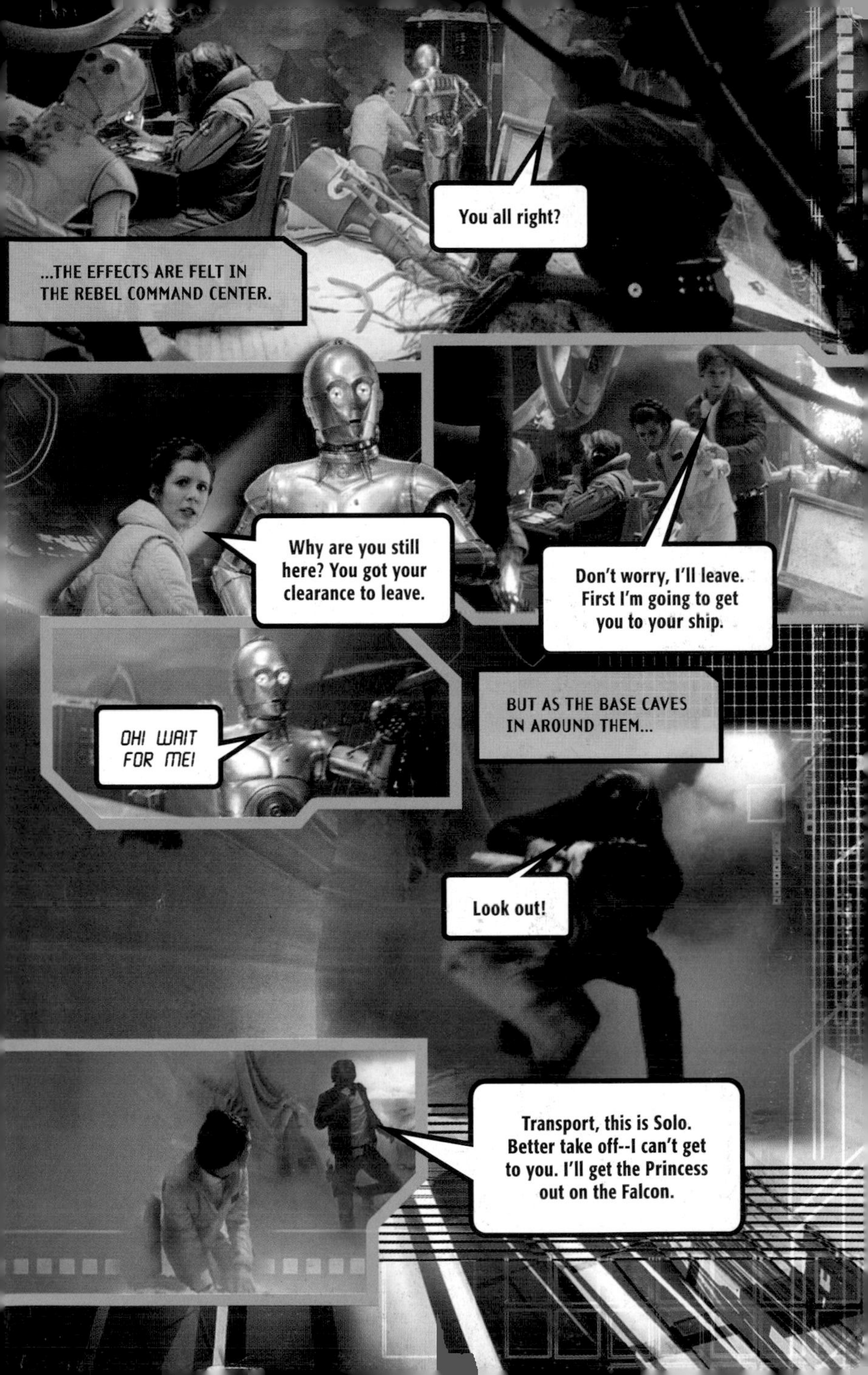

...THE EFFECTS ARE FELT IN THE REBEL COMMAND CENTER.
You all right?
Why are you still here? You got your clearance to leave.
Don't worry, I'll leave. First I'm going to get you to your ship.
OH! WAIT FOR ME!
BUT AS THE BASE CAVES IN AROUND THEM...
Look out!
Transport, this is Solo. Better take off--I can't get to you. I'll get the Princess out on the Falcon.

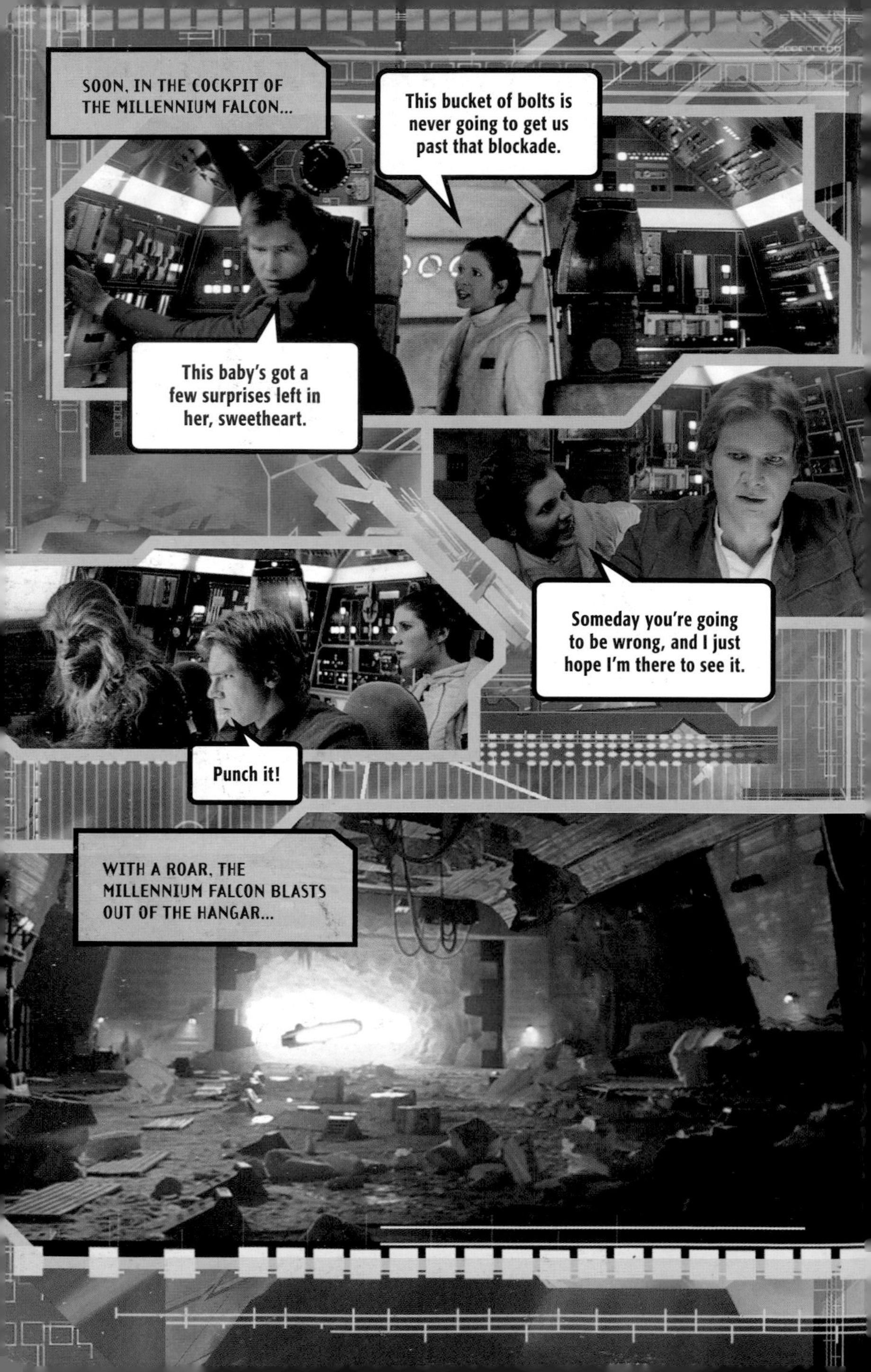

SOON, IN THE COCKPIT OF THE MILLENNIUM FALCON...
This bucket of bolts is never going to get us past that blockade.
This baby's got a few surprises left in her, sweetheart.
Someday you're going to be wrong, and I just hope I'm there to see it.
Punch it!
WITH A ROAR, THE MILLENNIUM FALCON BLASTS OUT OF THE HANGAR...

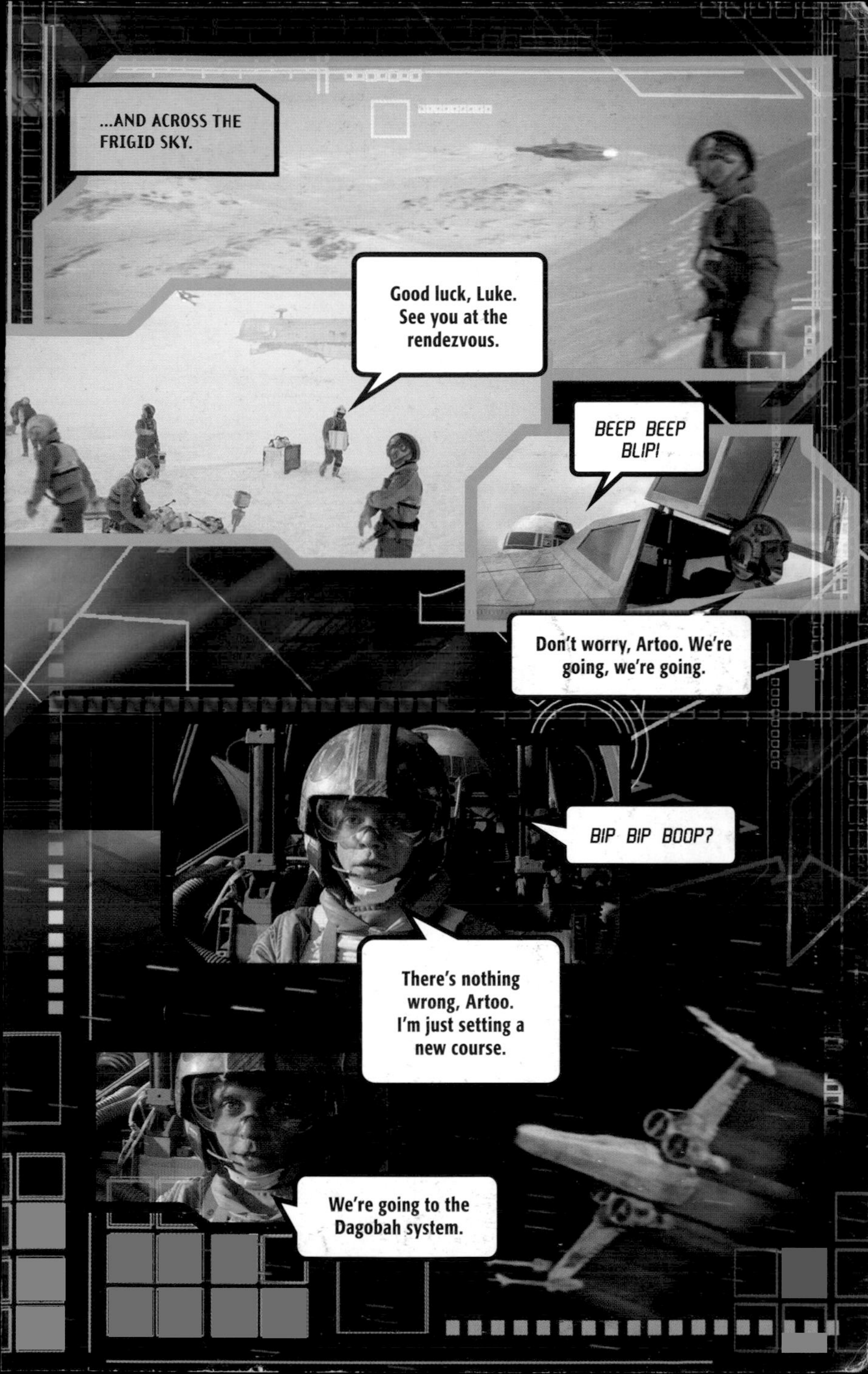
...AND ACROSS THE FRIGID SKY.
Good luck, Luke. See you at the rendezvous.
BEEP BEEP BLIP!
Don't worry, Artoo. We're going, we're going.
BIP BIP BOOP?
There's nothing wrong, Artoo. I'm just setting a new course.
We're going to the Dagobah system.

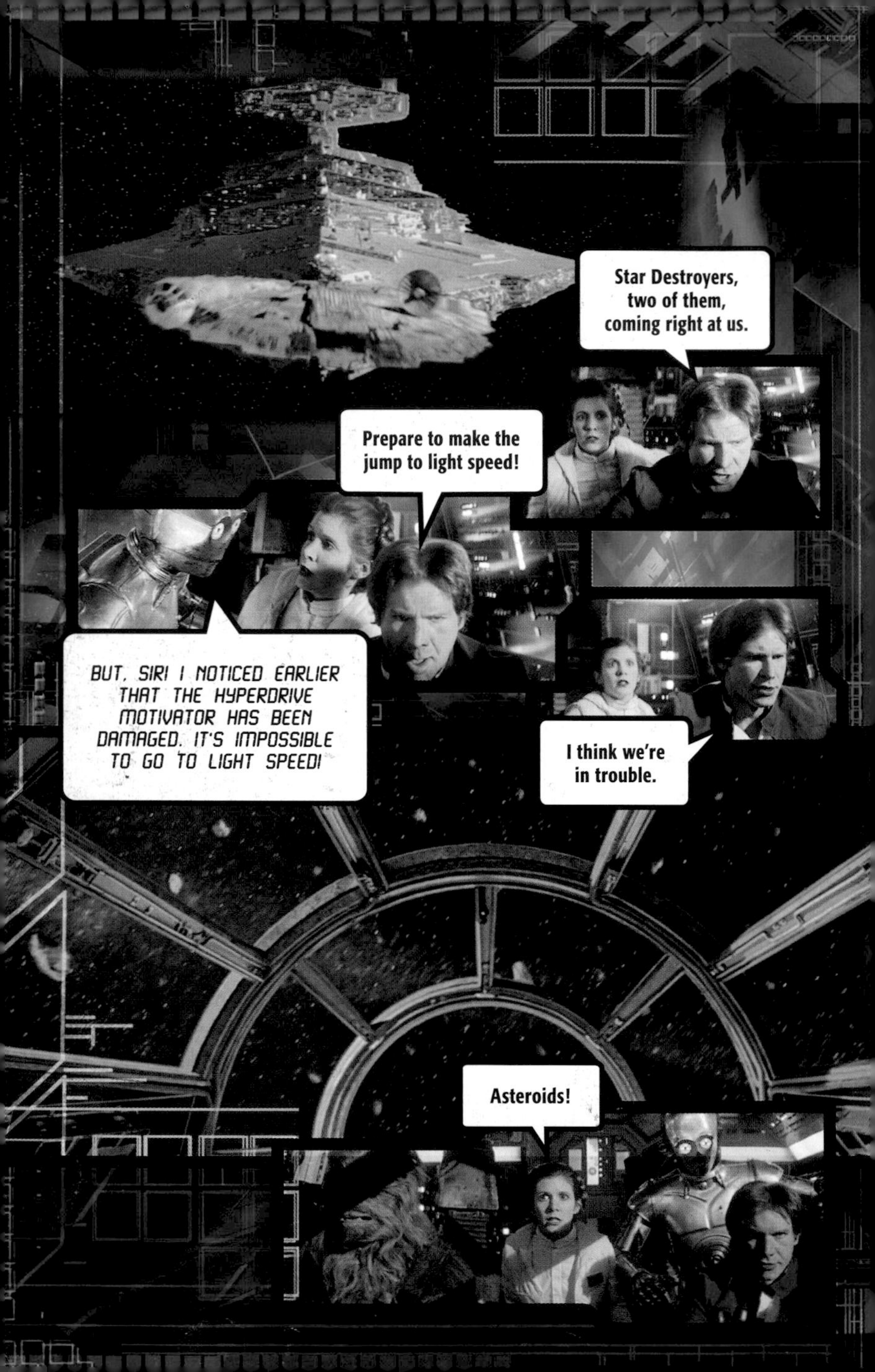
Star Destroyers, two of them, coming right at us.
Prepare to make the jump to light speed!
BUT, SIR! I NOTICED EARLIER THAT THE HYPERDRIVE MOTIVATOR HAS BEEN DAMAGED. IT'S IMPOSSIBLE TO GO TO LIGHT SPEED!
I think we're in trouble.
Asteroids!

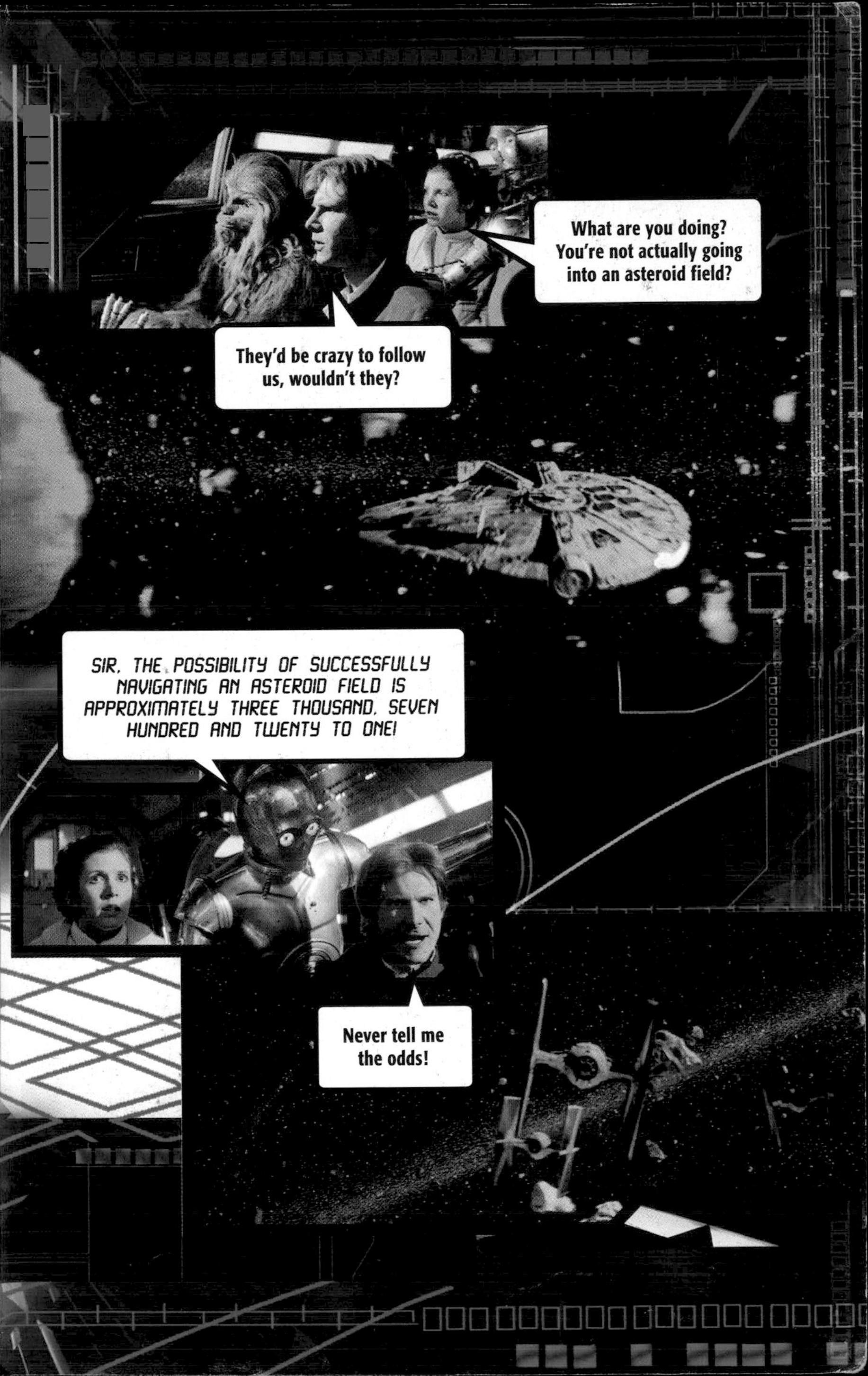
What are you doing? You're not actually going into an asteroid field?
They'd be crazy to follow us, wouldn't they?
SIR, THE POSSIBILITY OF SUCCESSFULLY NAVIGATING AN ASTEROID FIELD IS APPROXIMATELY THREE THOUSAND, SEVEN HUNDRED AND TWENTY TO ONE!
Never tell me the odds!

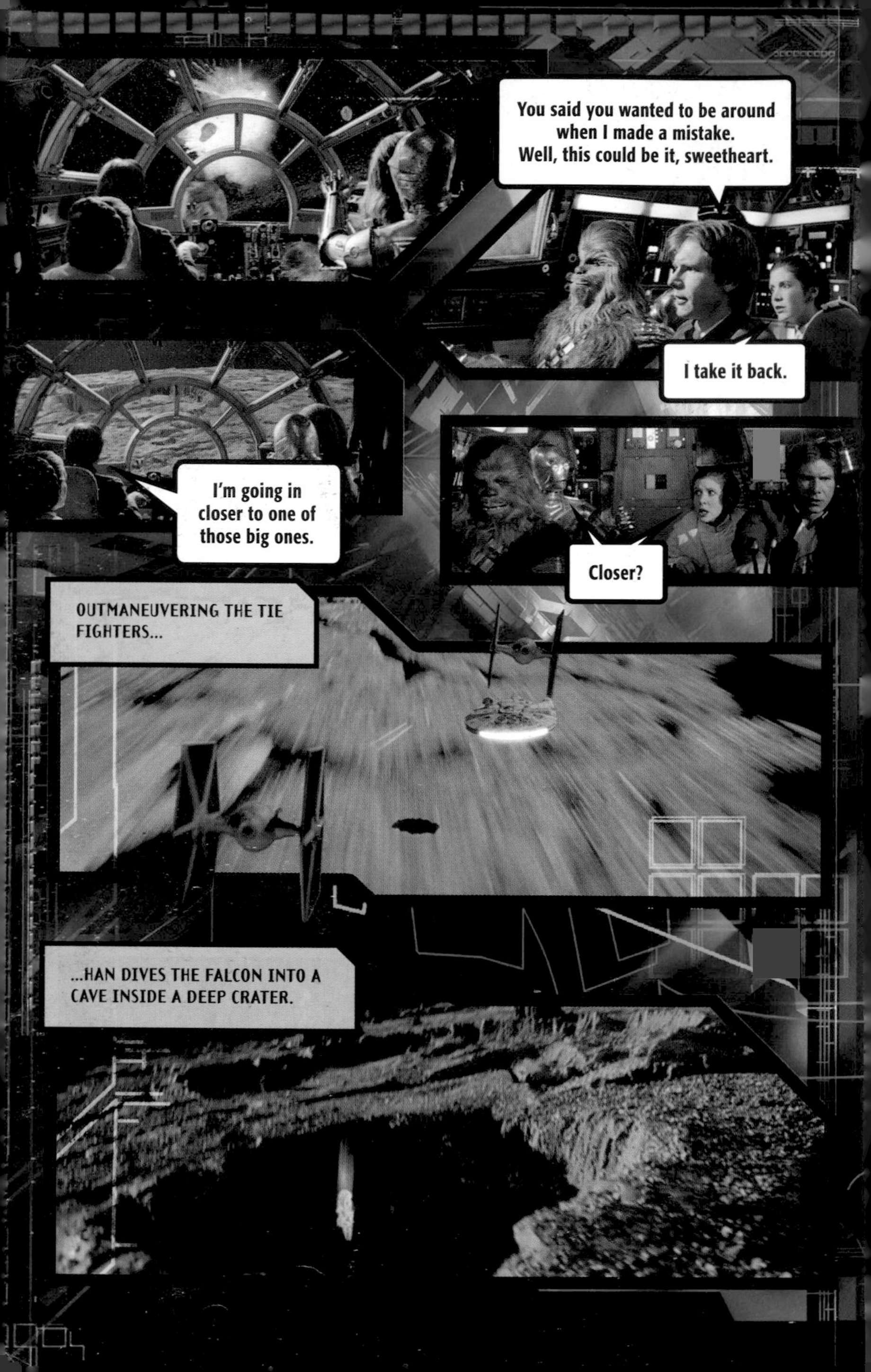
You said you wanted to be around when I made a mistake. Well, this could be it, sweetheart.
I take it back.
I'm going in closer to one of those big ones.
Closer?
OUTMANEUVERING THE TIE FIGHTERS...
...HAN DIVES THE FALCON INTO A CAVE INSIDE A DEEP CRATER.

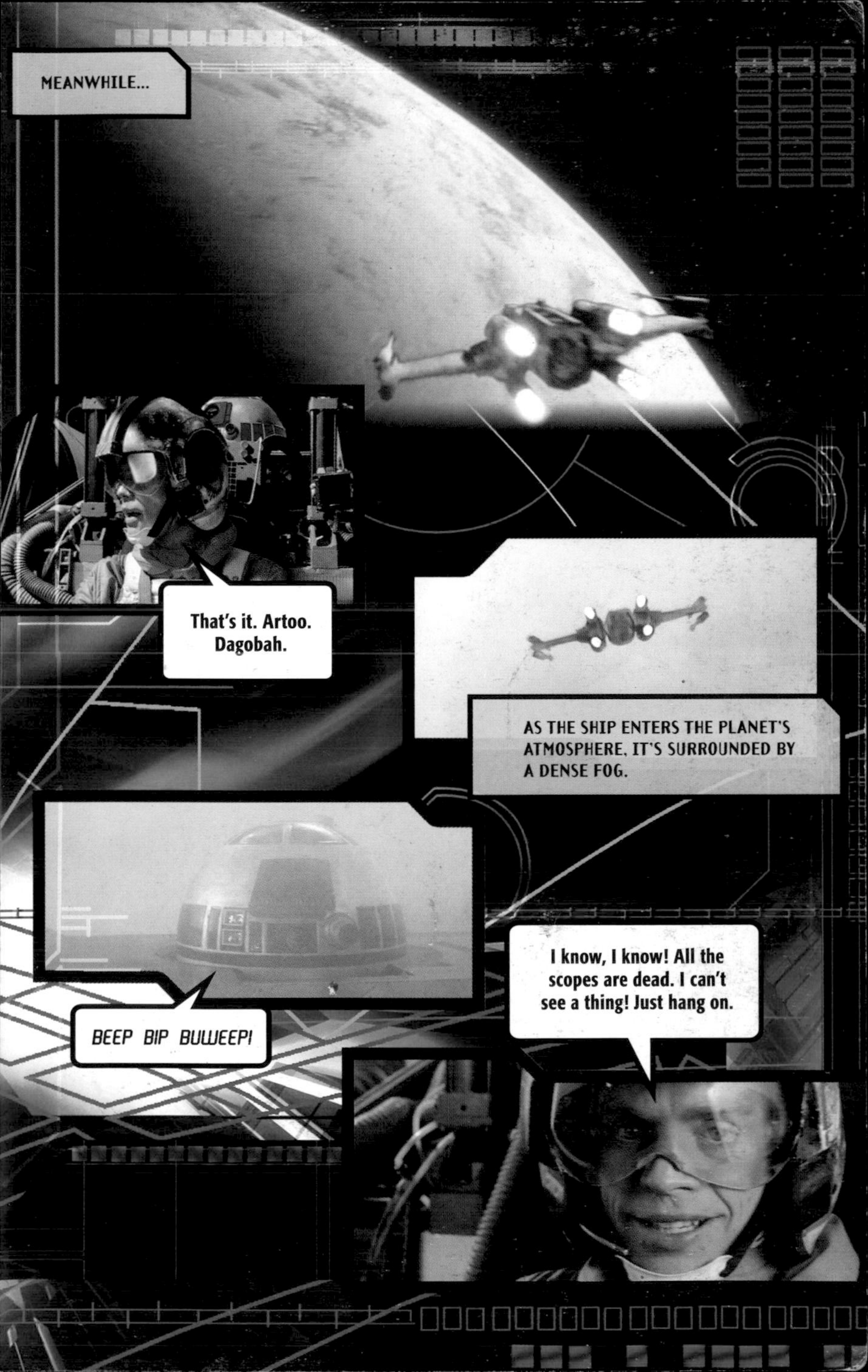
MEANWHILE...
That's it. Artoo. Dagobah.
AS THE SHIP ENTERS THE PLANET'S ATMOSPHERE, IT'S SURROUNDED BY A DENSE FOG.
BEEP BIP BUWEEP!
I know, I know! All the scopes are dead. I can't see a thing! Just hang on.

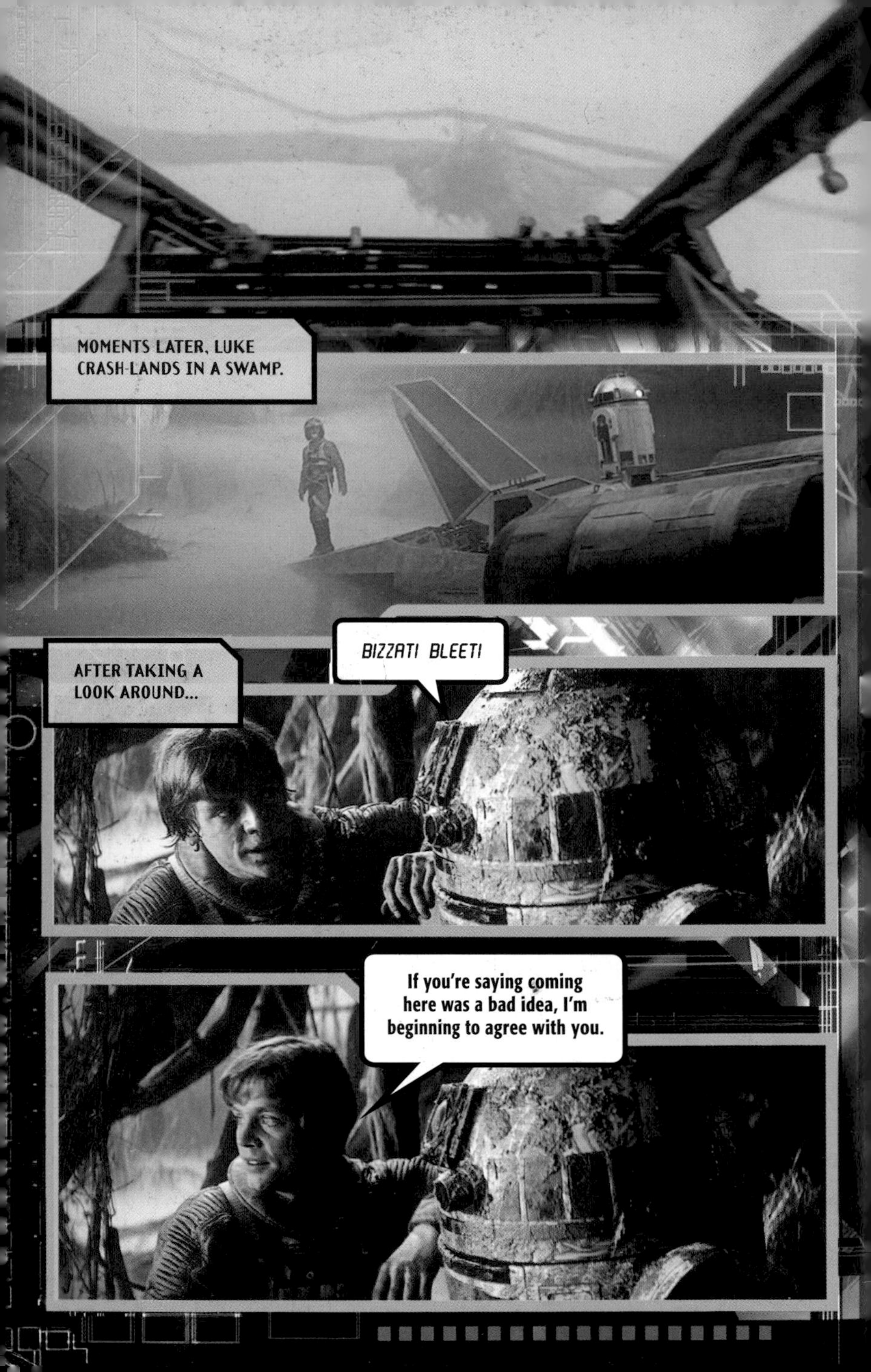
MOMENTS LATER, LUKE CRASH-LANDS IN A SWAMP.
AFTER TAKING A LOOK AROUND...
BIZZATI BLEET!
If you're saying coming here was a bad idea, I'm beginning to agree with you.

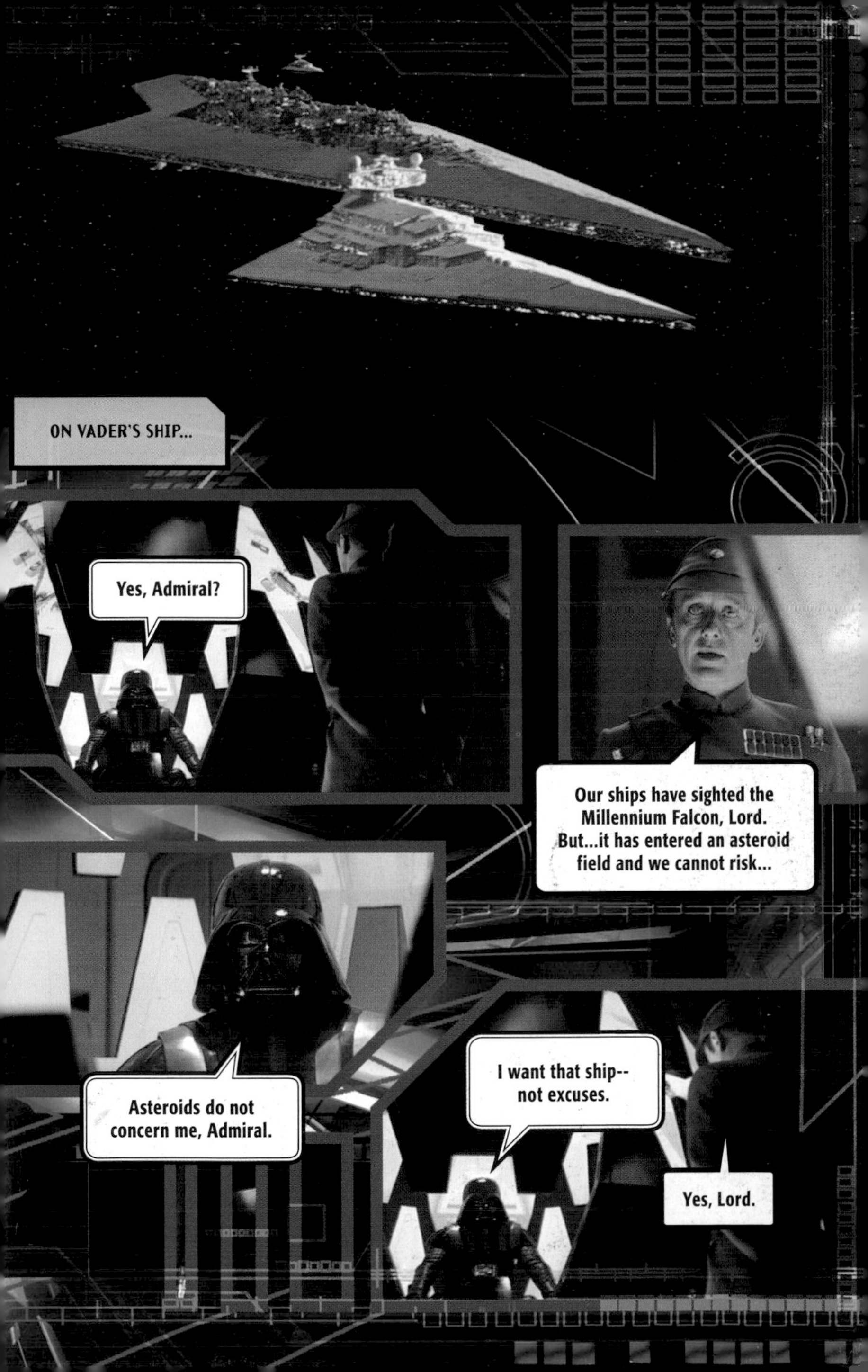
ON VADER'S SHIP...
Yes, Admiral?
Our ships have sighted the Millennium Falcon, Lord. But...it has entered an asteroid field and we cannot risk...
Asteroids do not concern me, Admiral.
I want that ship-- not excuses.
Yes, Lord.

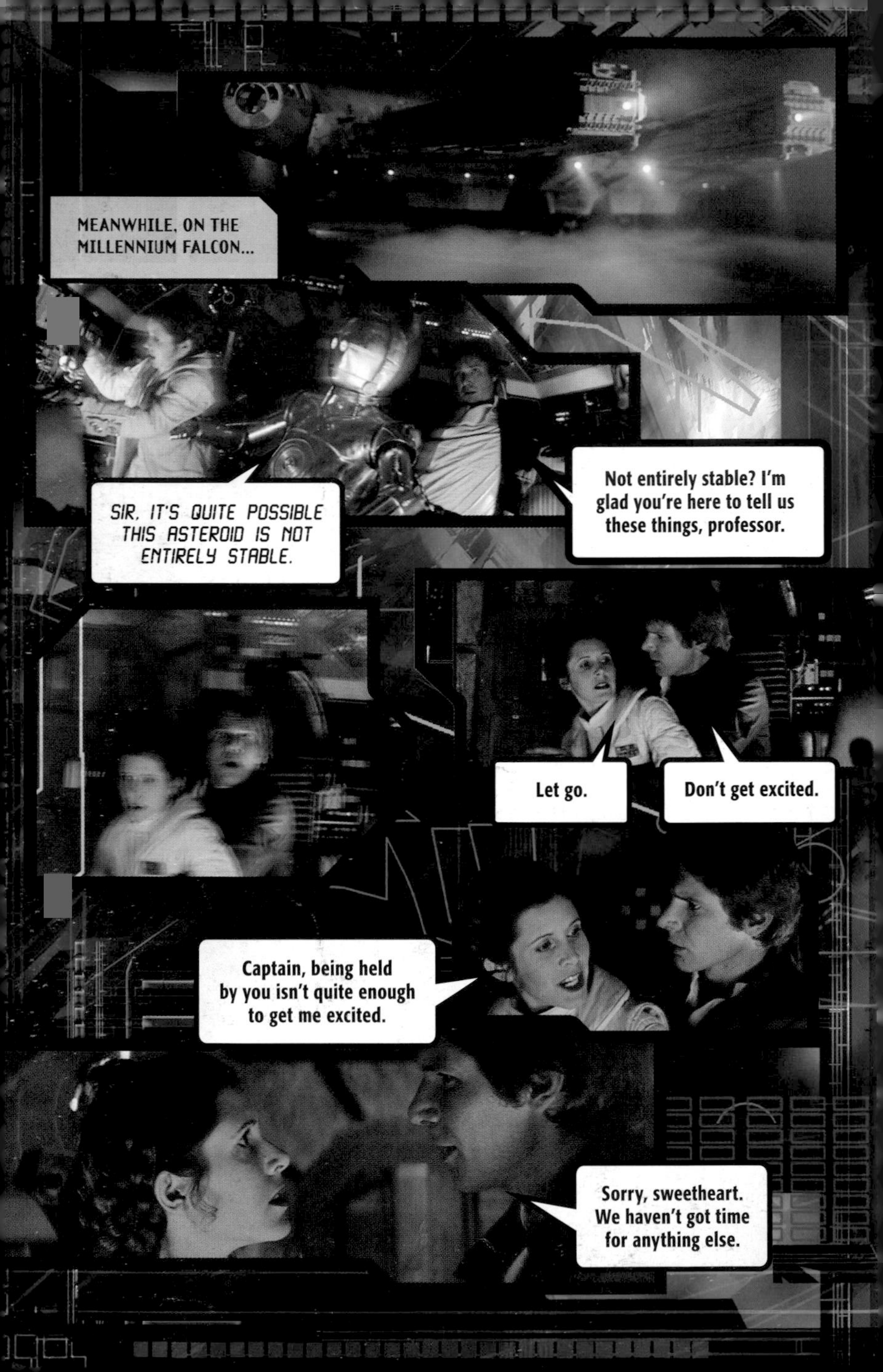
MEANWHILE, ON THE MILLENNIUM FALCON...
SIR, IT'S QUITE POSSIBLE THIS ASTEROID IS NOT ENTIRELY STABLE.
Not entirely stable? I'm glad you're here to tell us these things, professor.
Let go.
Don't get excited.
Captain, being held by you isn't quite enough to get me excited.
Sorry, sweetheart. We haven't got time for anything else.

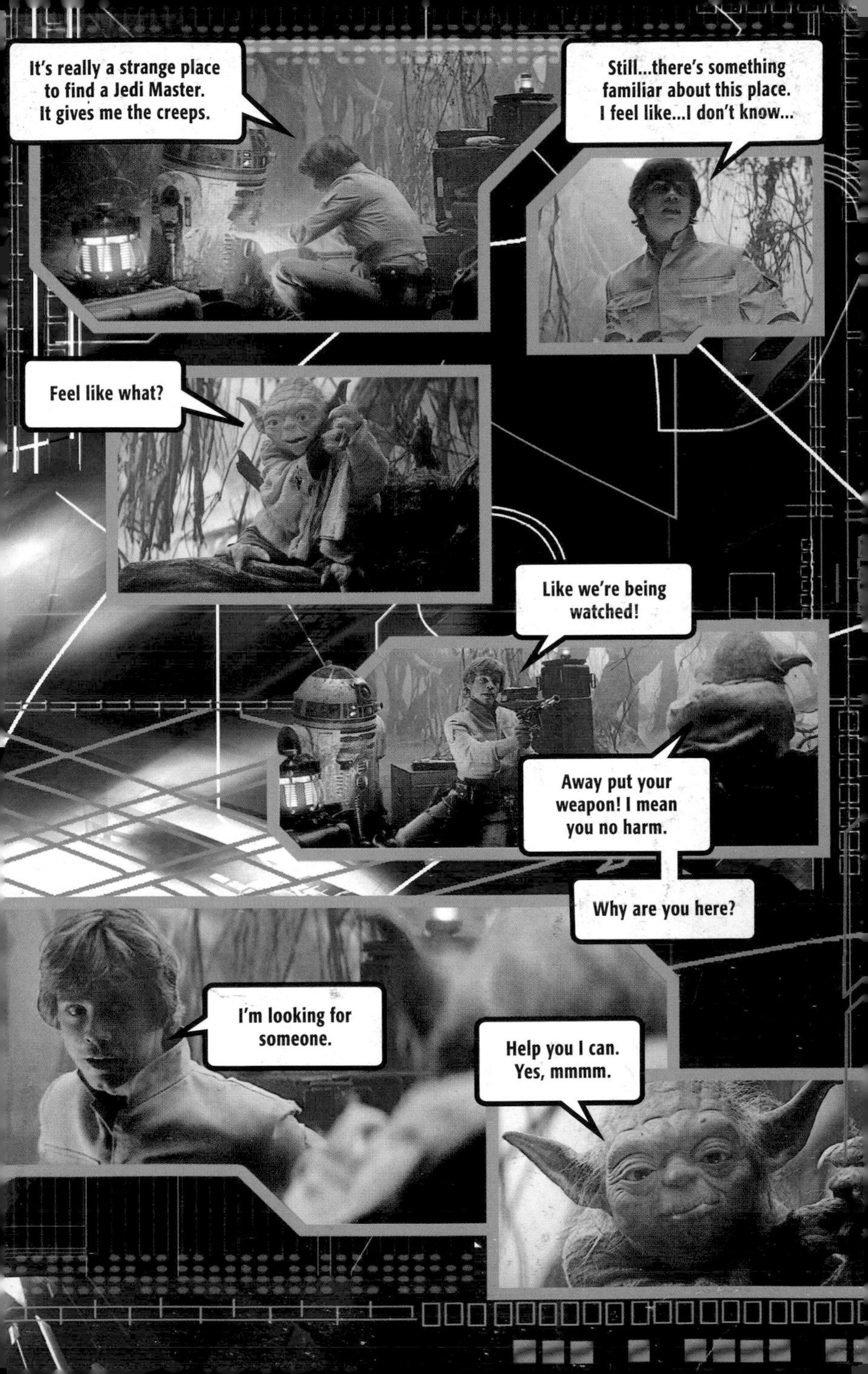
It's really a strange place to find a Jedi Master. It gives me the creeps.
Still...there's something familiar about this place. I feel like...I don't know...
Feel like what?
Like we're being watched!
Away put your weapon! I mean you no harm.
Why are you here?
I'm looking for someone.
Help you I can. Yes, mmmm.

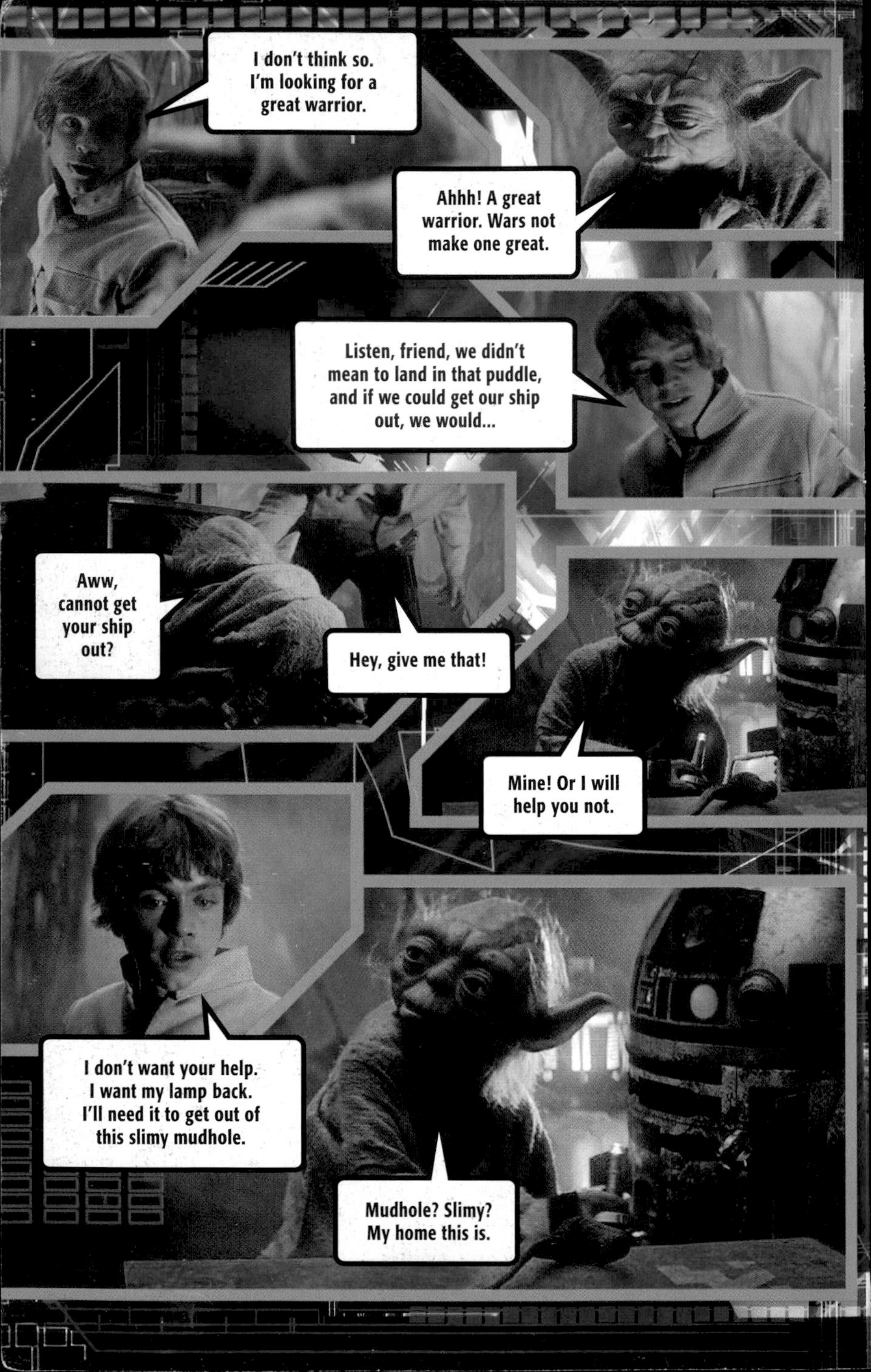
I don't think so. I'm looking for a great warrior.
Ahhh! A great warrior. Wars not make one great.
Listen, friend, we didn't mean to land in that puddle, and if we could get our ship out, we would...
Aww, cannot get your ship out?
Hey, give me that!
Mine! Or I will help you not.
I don't want your help. I want my lamp back. I'll need it to get out of this slimy mudhole.
Mudhole? Slimy? My home this is.

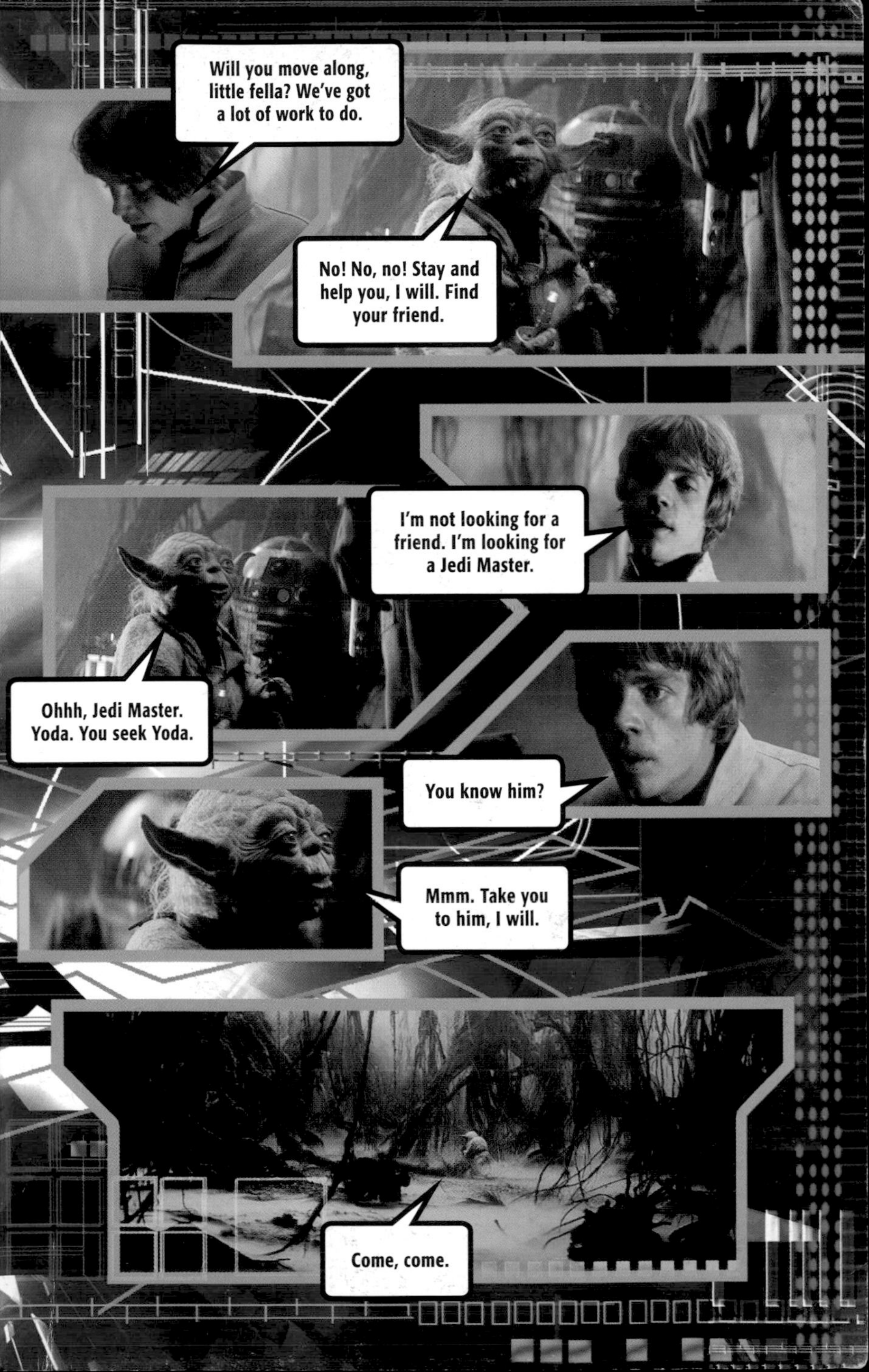
Will you move along, little fella? We've got a lot of work to do.
No! No, no! Stay and help you, I will. Find your friend.
I'm not looking for a friend. I'm looking for a Jedi Master.
Ohhh, Jedi Master. Yoda. You seek Yoda.
You know him?
Mmm. Take you to him, I will.
Come, come.

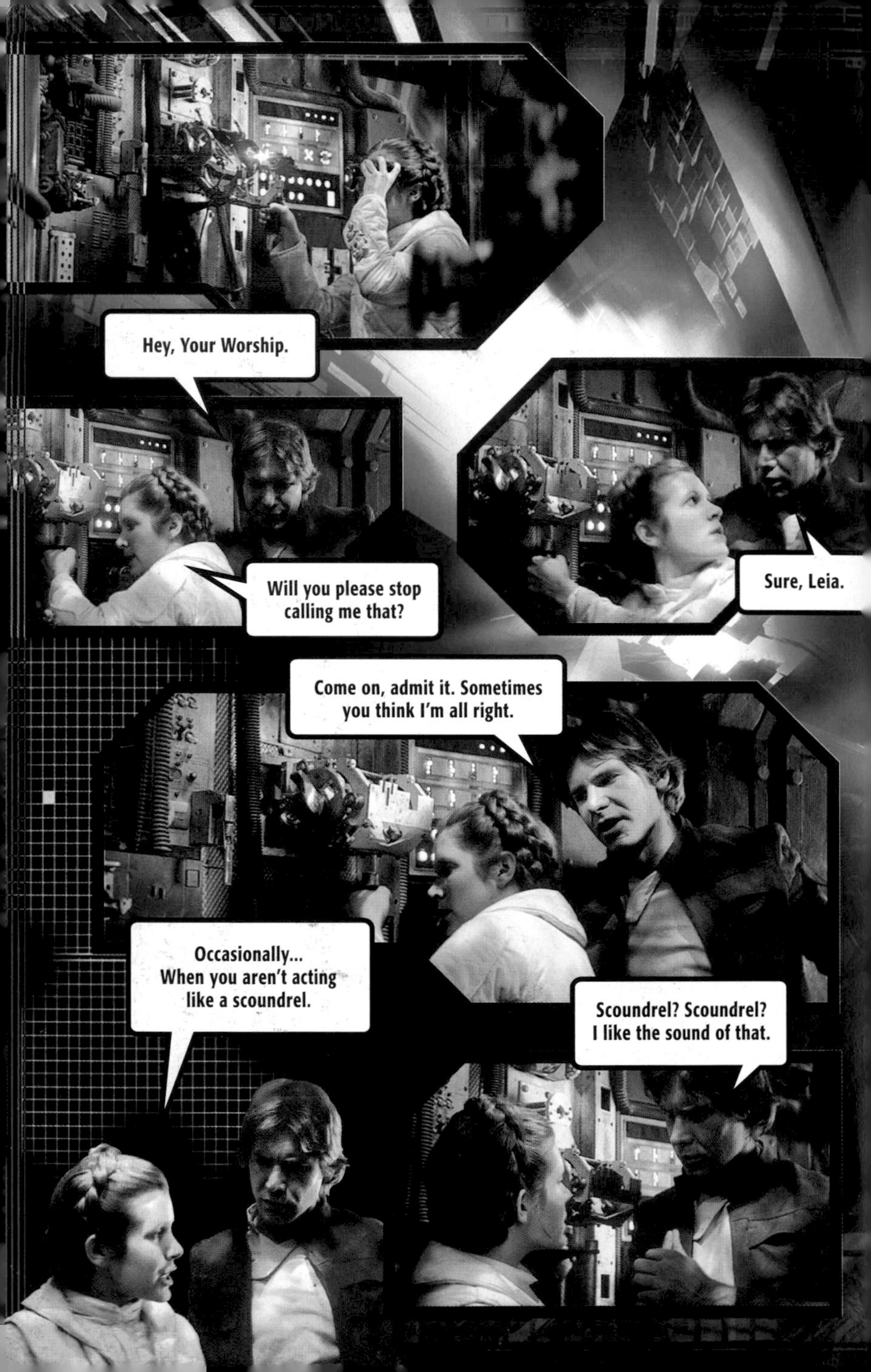
Hey, Your Worship.
Will you please stop calling me that?
Sure, Leia.
Come on, admit it. Sometimes you think I'm all right.
Occasionally... When you aren't acting like a scoundrel.
Scoundrel? Scoundrel? I like the sound of that.

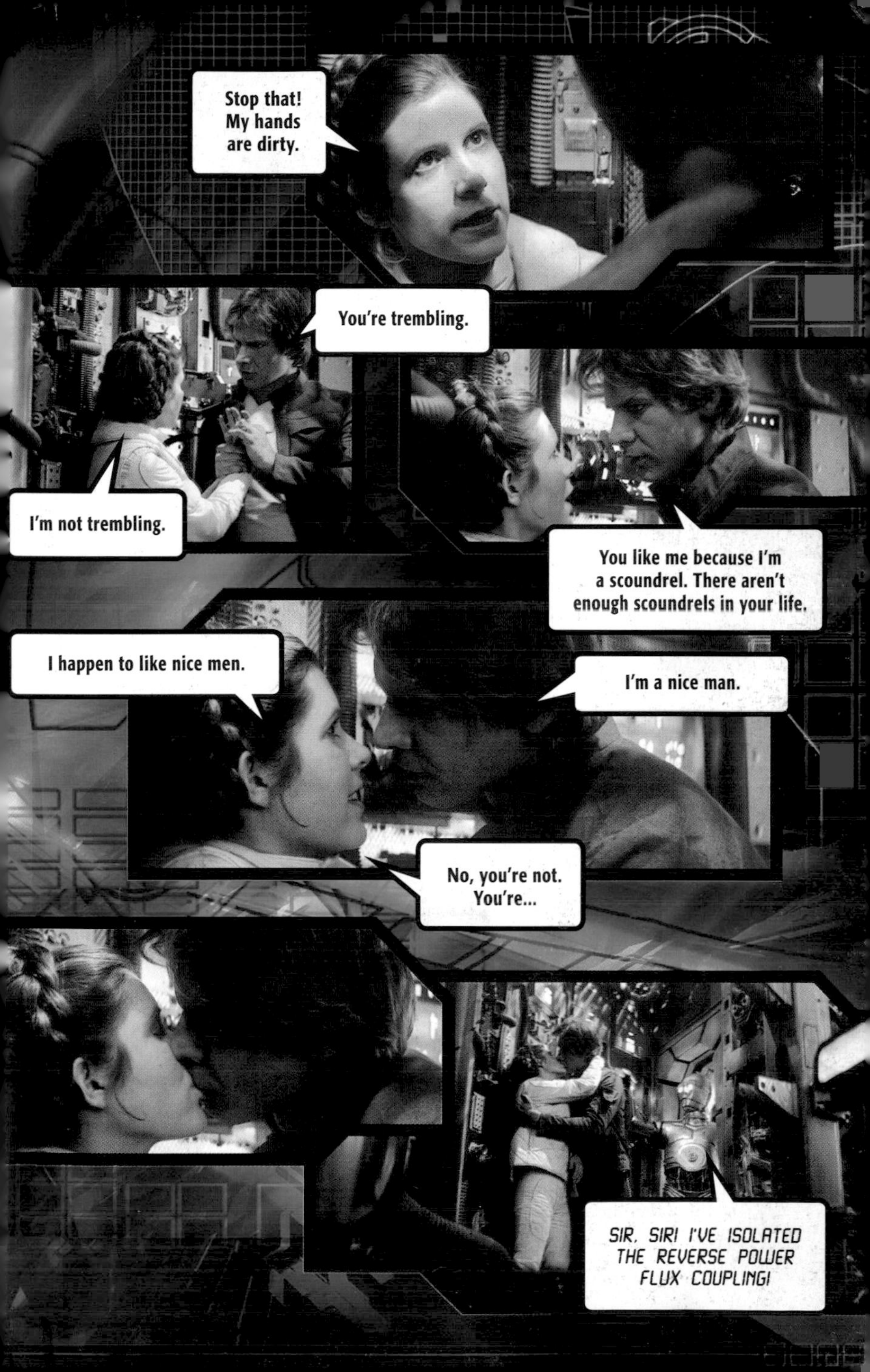
Stop that! My hands are dirty.
You're trembling.
I'm not trembling.
You like me because I'm a scoundrel. There aren't enough scoundrels in your life.
I happen to like nice men.
I'm a nice man.
No, you're not. You're...
SIR, SIR! I'VE ISOLATED THE REVERSE POWER FLUX COUPLING!

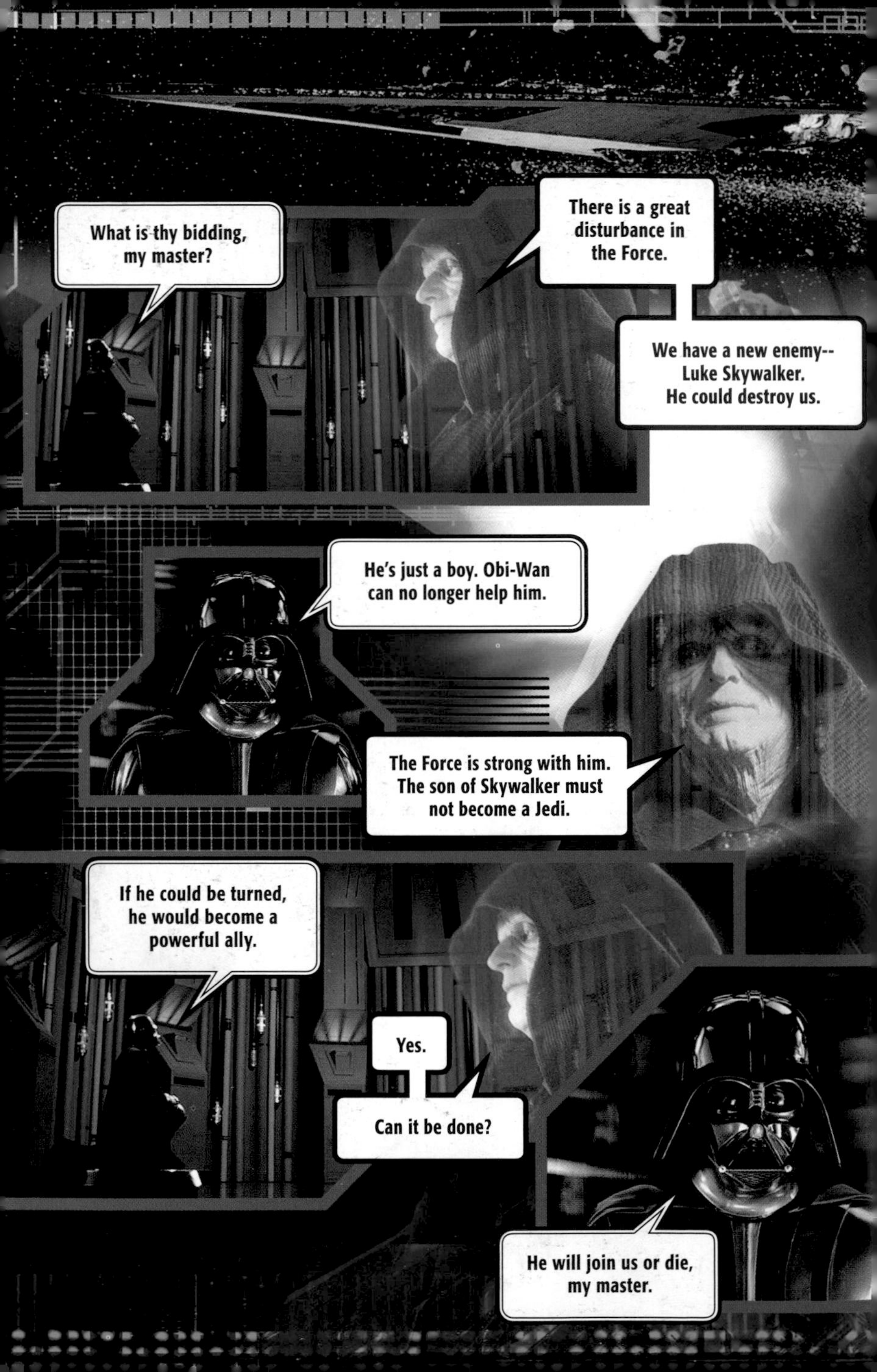
What is thy bidding, my master?
There is a great disturbance in the Force.
We have a new enemy--
Luke Skywalker.
He could destroy us.
He's just a boy. Obi-Wan can no longer help him.
The Force is strong with him. The son of Skywalker must not become a Jedi.
If he could be turned, he would become a powerful ally.
Yes.
Can it be done?
He will join us or die, my master.

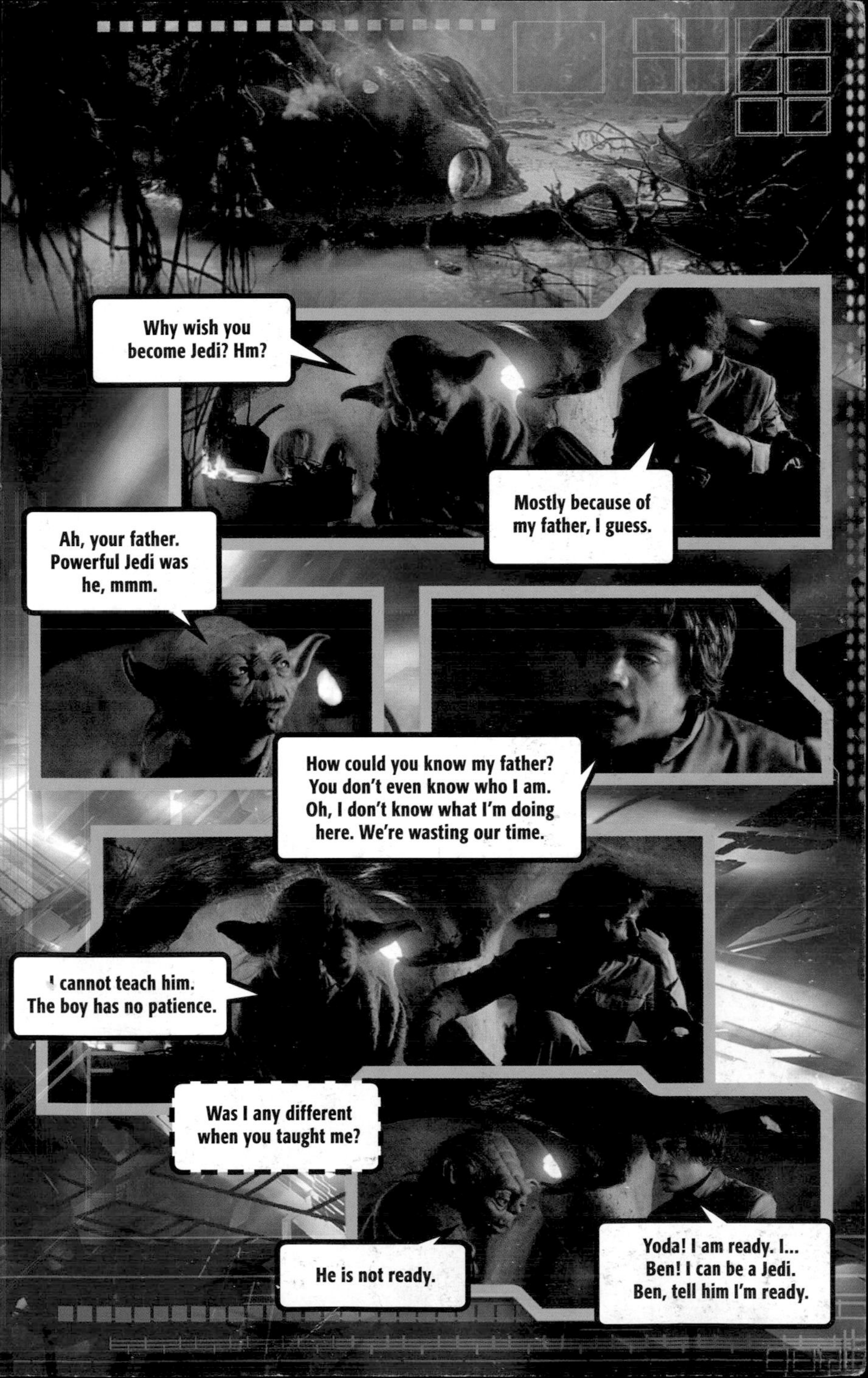
Why wish you become Jedi? Hm?
Mostly because of my father, I guess.
Ah, your father. Powerful Jedi was he, mmm.
How could you know my father? You don't even know who I am. Oh, I don't know what I'm doing here. We're wasting our time.
I cannot teach him. The boy has no patience.
Was I any different when you taught me?
He is not ready.
Yoda! I am ready. I... Ben! I can be a Jedi. Ben, tell him I'm ready.

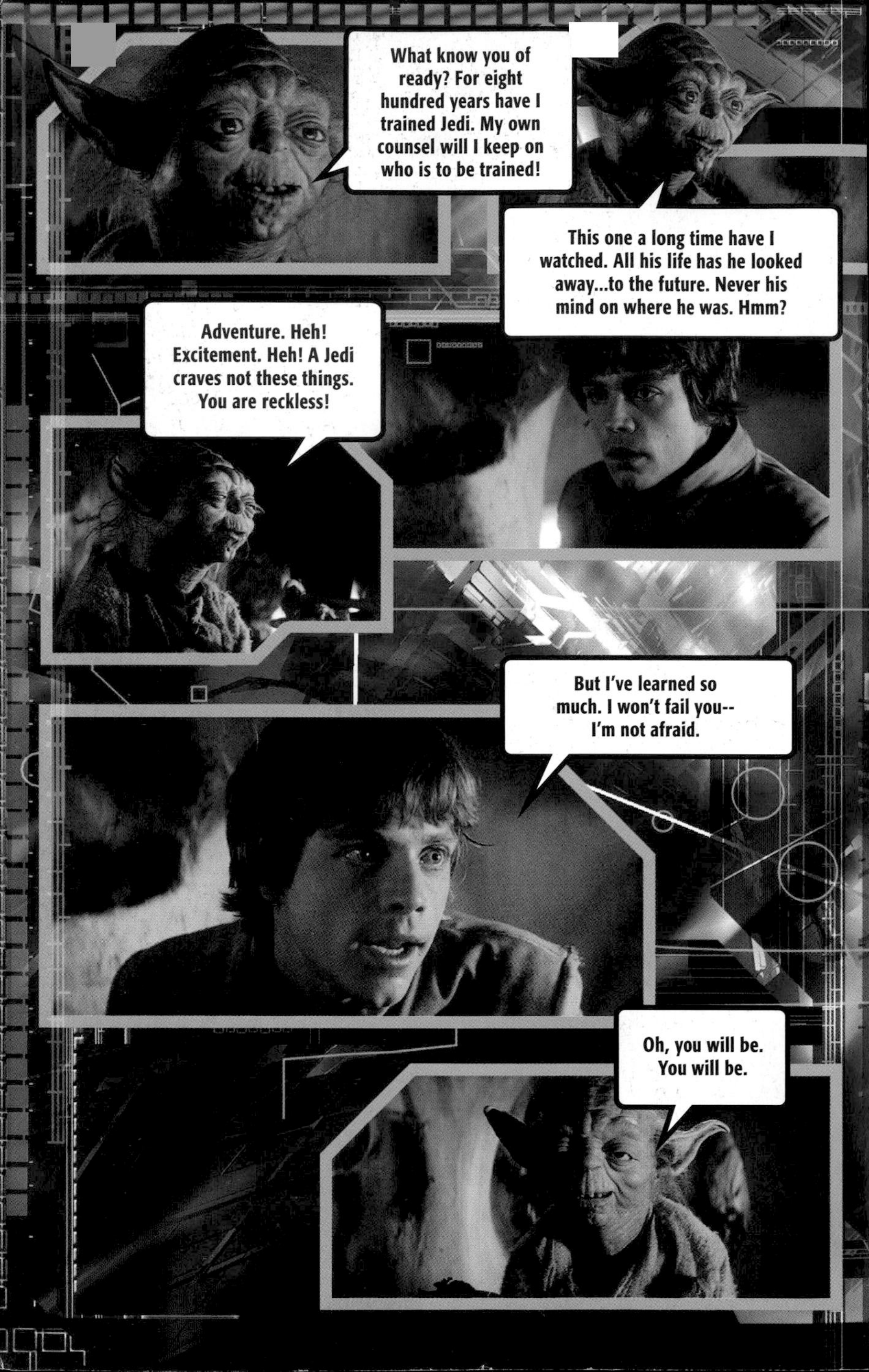
What know you of ready? For eight hundred years have I trained Jedi. My own counsel will I keep on who is to be trained!
This one a long time have I watched. All his life has he looked away...to the future. Never his mind on where he was. Hmm?
Adventure. Heh! Excitement. Heh! A Jedi craves not these things. You are reckless!
But I've learned so much. I won't fail you-- I'm not afraid.
Oh, you will be. You will be.

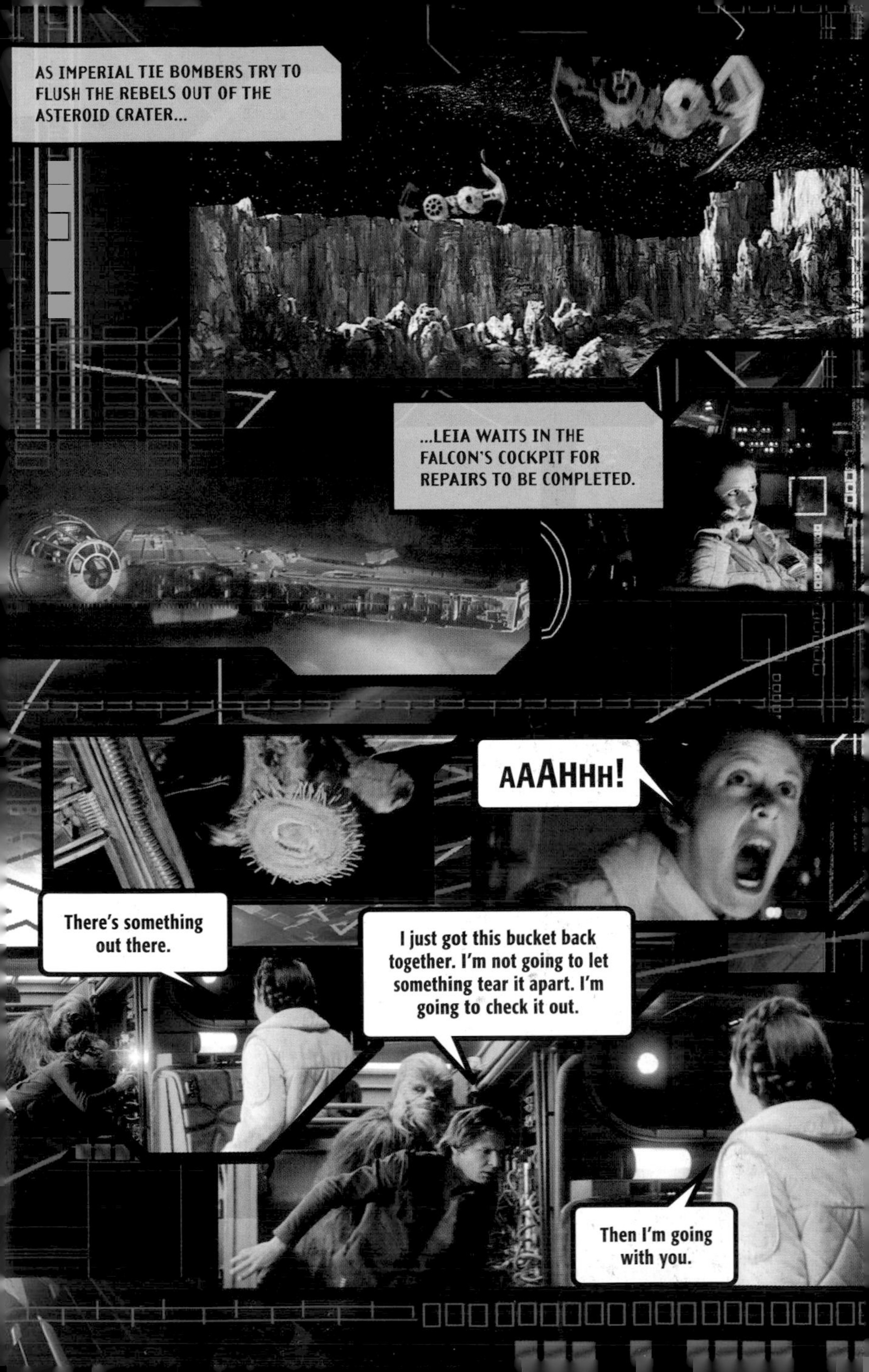
AS IMPERIAL TIE BOMBERS TRY TO FLUSH THE REBELS OUT OF THE ASTEROID CRATER...
...LEIA WAITS IN THE FALCON'S COCKPIT FOR REPAIRS TO BE COMPLETED.
AAAHHH!
There's something out there.
I just got this bucket back together. I'm not going to let something tear it apart. I'm going to check it out.
Then I'm going with you.

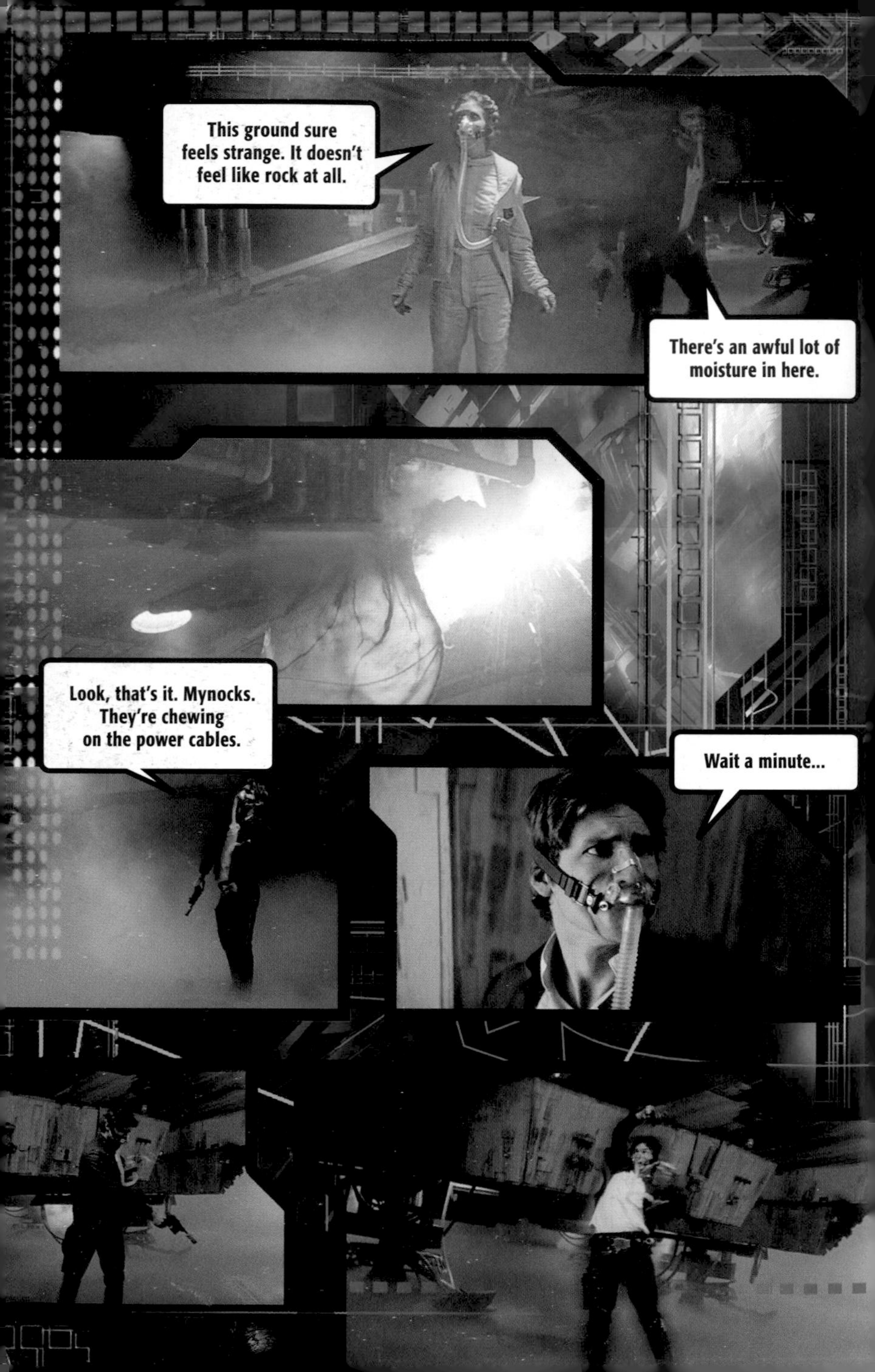
This ground sure feels strange. It doesn't feel like rock at all.
There's an awful lot of moisture in here.
Look, that's it. Mynocks. They're chewing on the power cables.
Wait a minute...

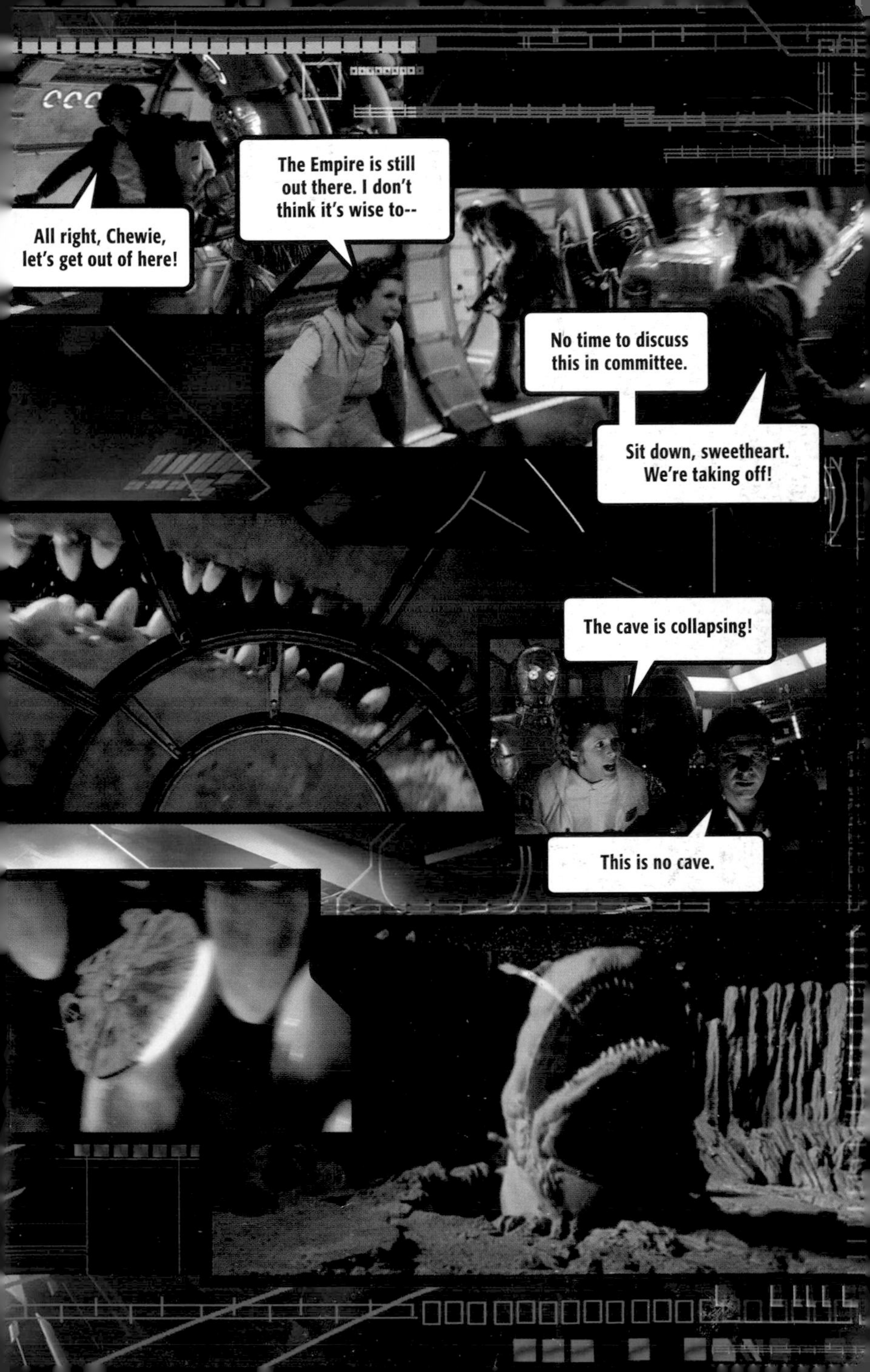

All right, Chewie, let's get out of here!
The Empire is still out there. I don't think it's wise to--
No time to discuss this in committee.
Sit down, sweetheart. We're taking off!
The cave is collapsing!
This is no cave.

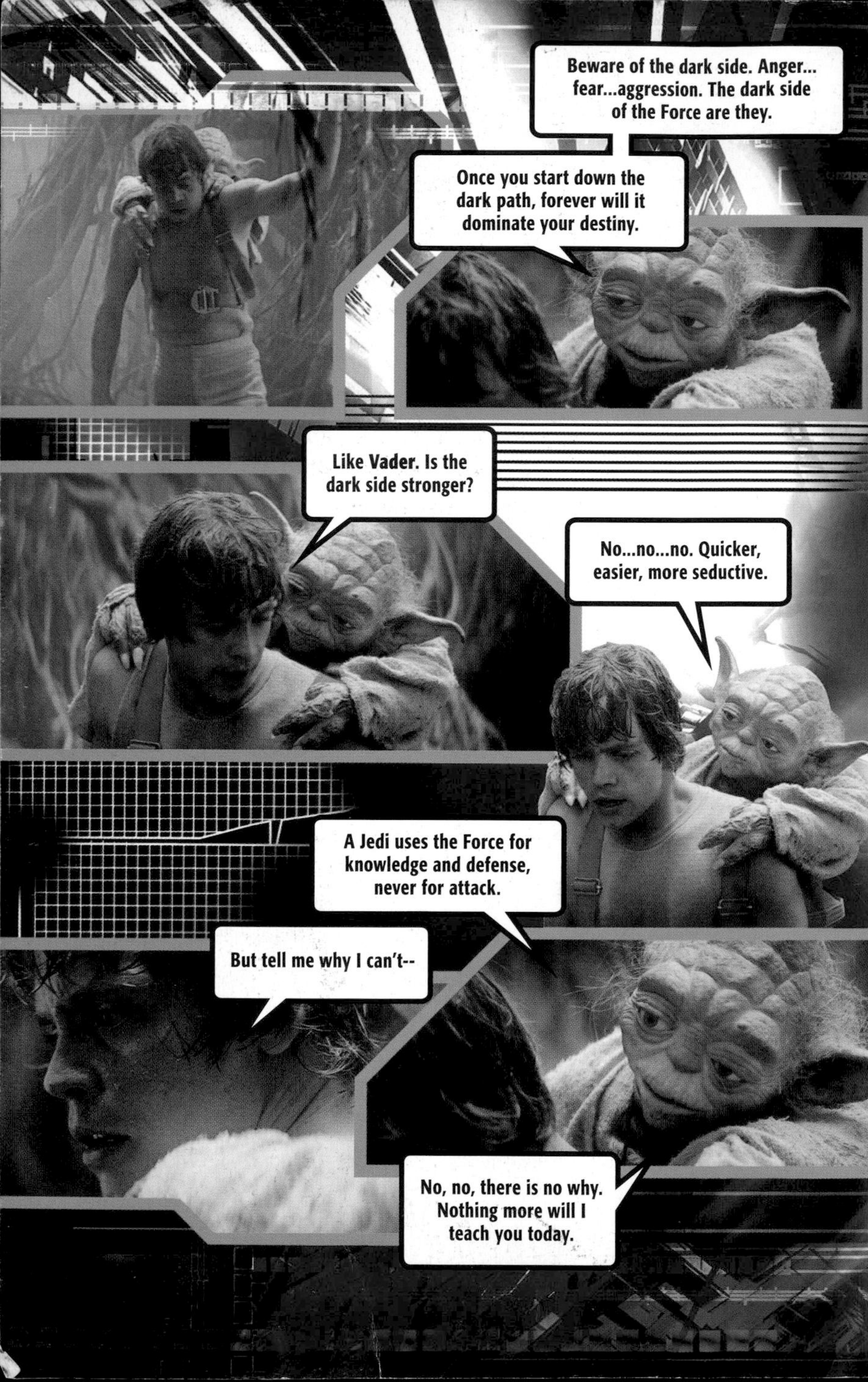
Beware of the dark side. Anger... fear...aggression. The dark side of the Force are they.
Once you start down the dark path, forever will it dominate your destiny.
Like Vader. Is the dark side stronger?
No...no...no. Quicker, easier, more seductive.
A Jedi uses the Force for knowledge and defense, never for attack.
But tell me why I can't--
No, no, there is no why. Nothing more will I teach you today.

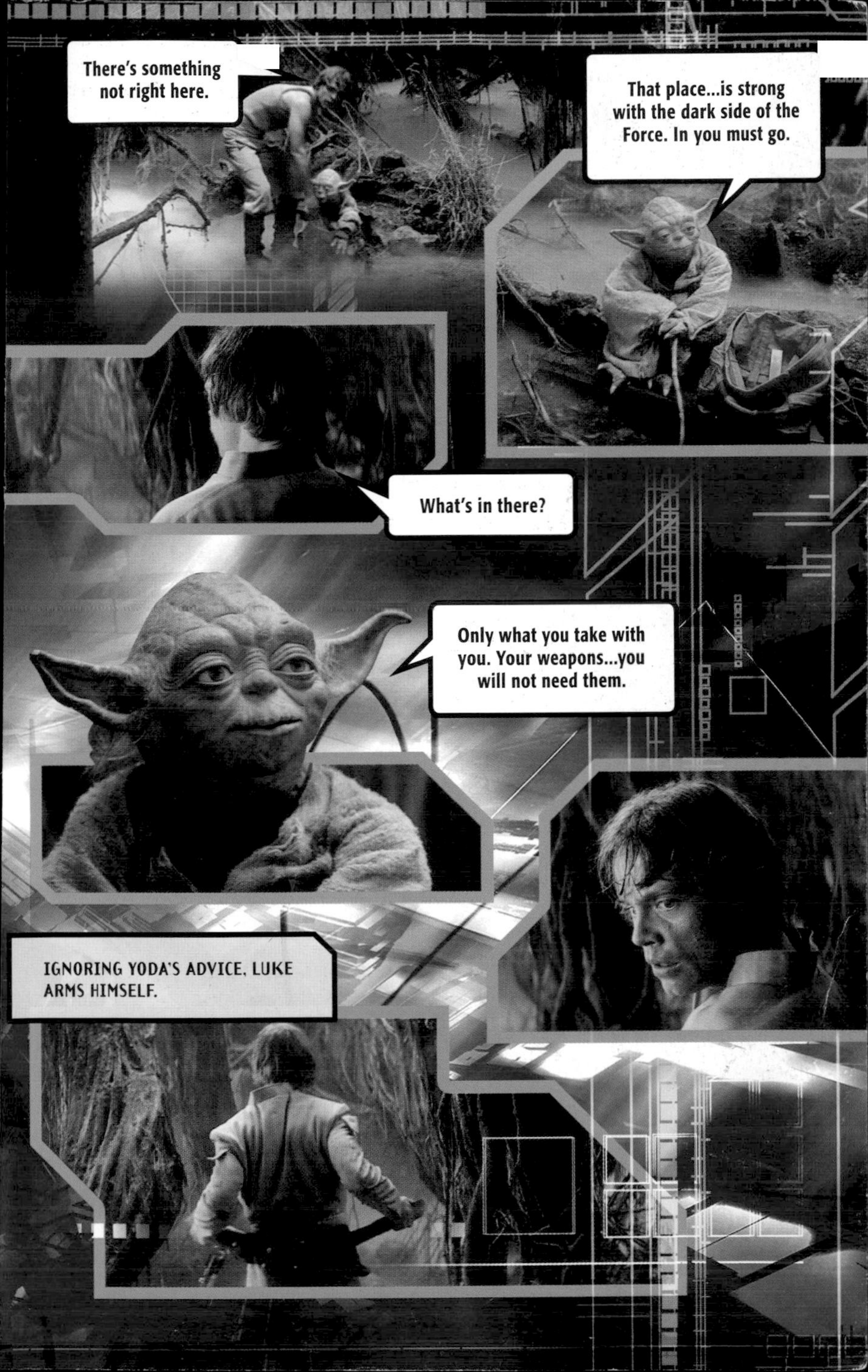
There's something not right here.
That place...is strong with the dark side of the Force. In you must go.
What's in there?
Only what you take with you. Your weapons...you will not need them.
IGNORING YODA'S ADVICE, LUKE ARMS HIMSELF.

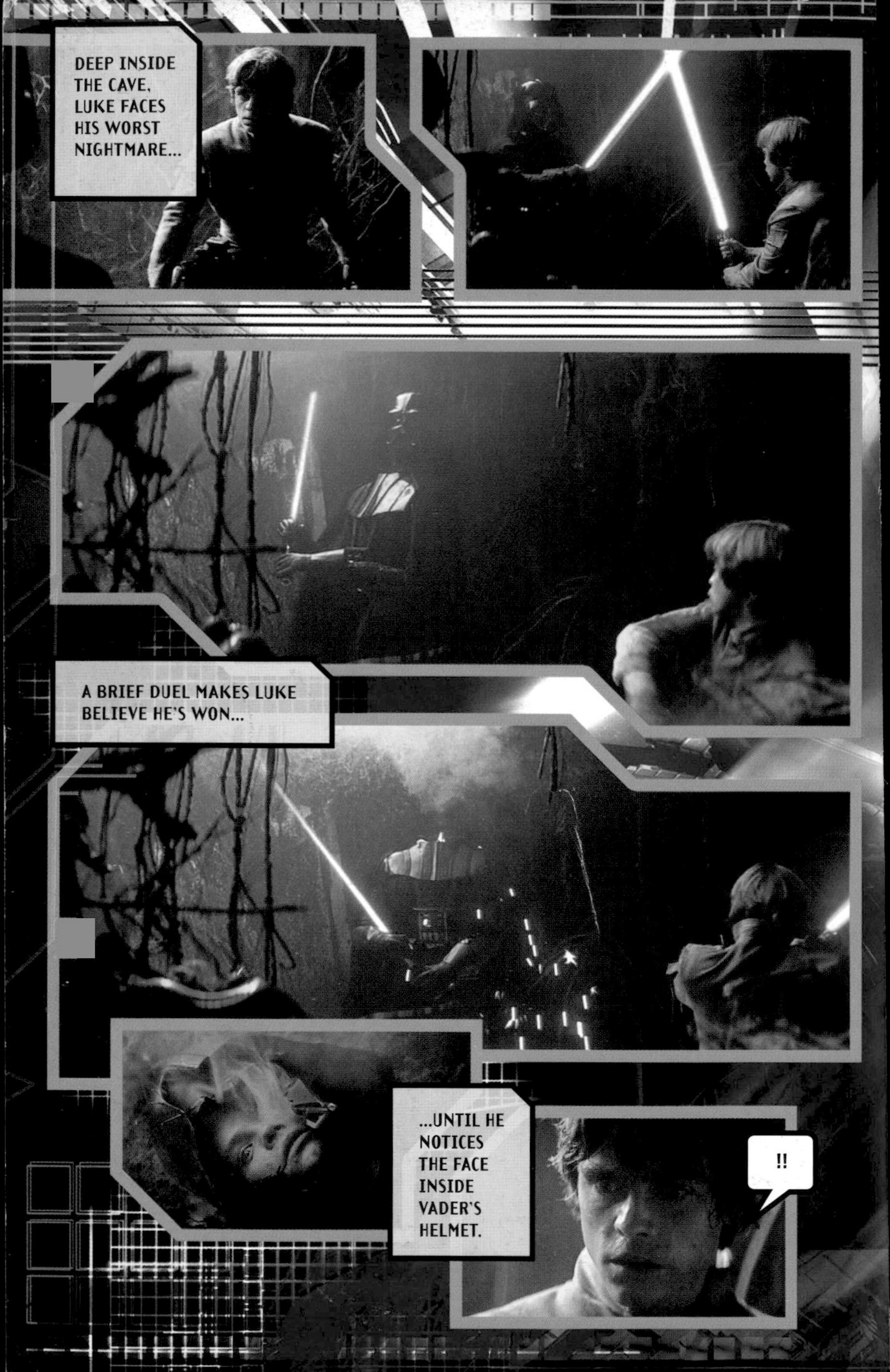
DEEP INSIDE THE CAVE, LUKE FACES HIS WORST NIGHTMARE...
A BRIEF DUEL MAKES LUKE BELIEVE HE'S WON...
...UNTIL HE NOTICES THE FACE INSIDE VADER'S HELMET.
!!

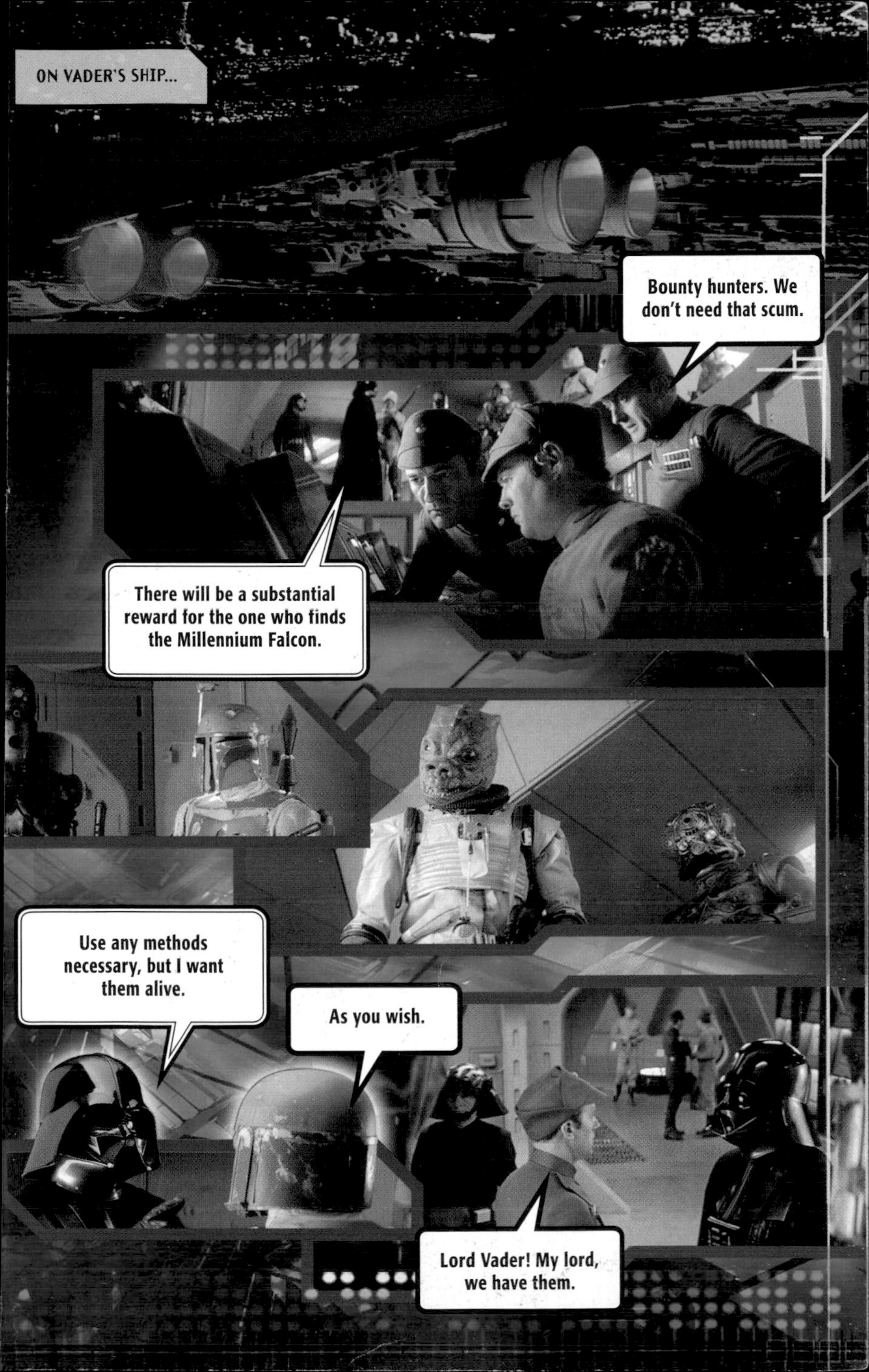
ON VADER'S SHIP...
Bounty hunters. We don't need that scum.
There will be a substantial reward for the one who finds the Millennium Falcon.
Use any methods necessary, but I want them alive.
As you wish.
Lord Vader! My lord, we have them.

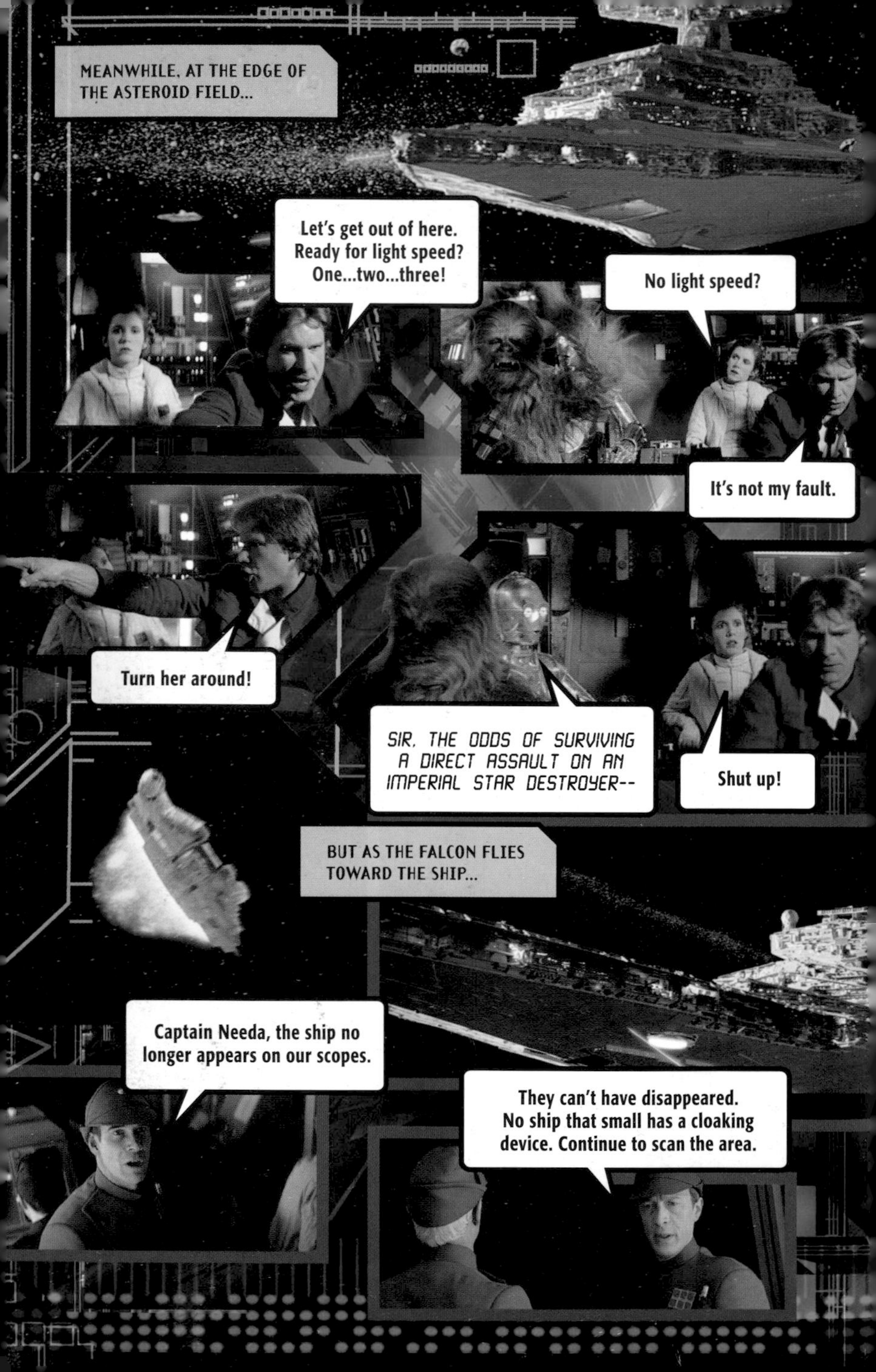
MEANWHILE, AT THE EDGE OF THE ASTEROID FIELD...
Let's get out of here. Ready for light speed? One...two...three!
No light speed?
It's not my fault.
Turn her around!
SIR, THE ODDS OF SURVIVING A DIRECT ASSAULT ON AN IMPERIAL STAR DESTROYER--
Shut up!
BUT AS THE FALCON FLIES TOWARD THE SHIP...
Captain Needa, the ship no longer appears on our scopes.
They can't have disappeared. No ship that small has a cloaking device. Continue to scan the area.

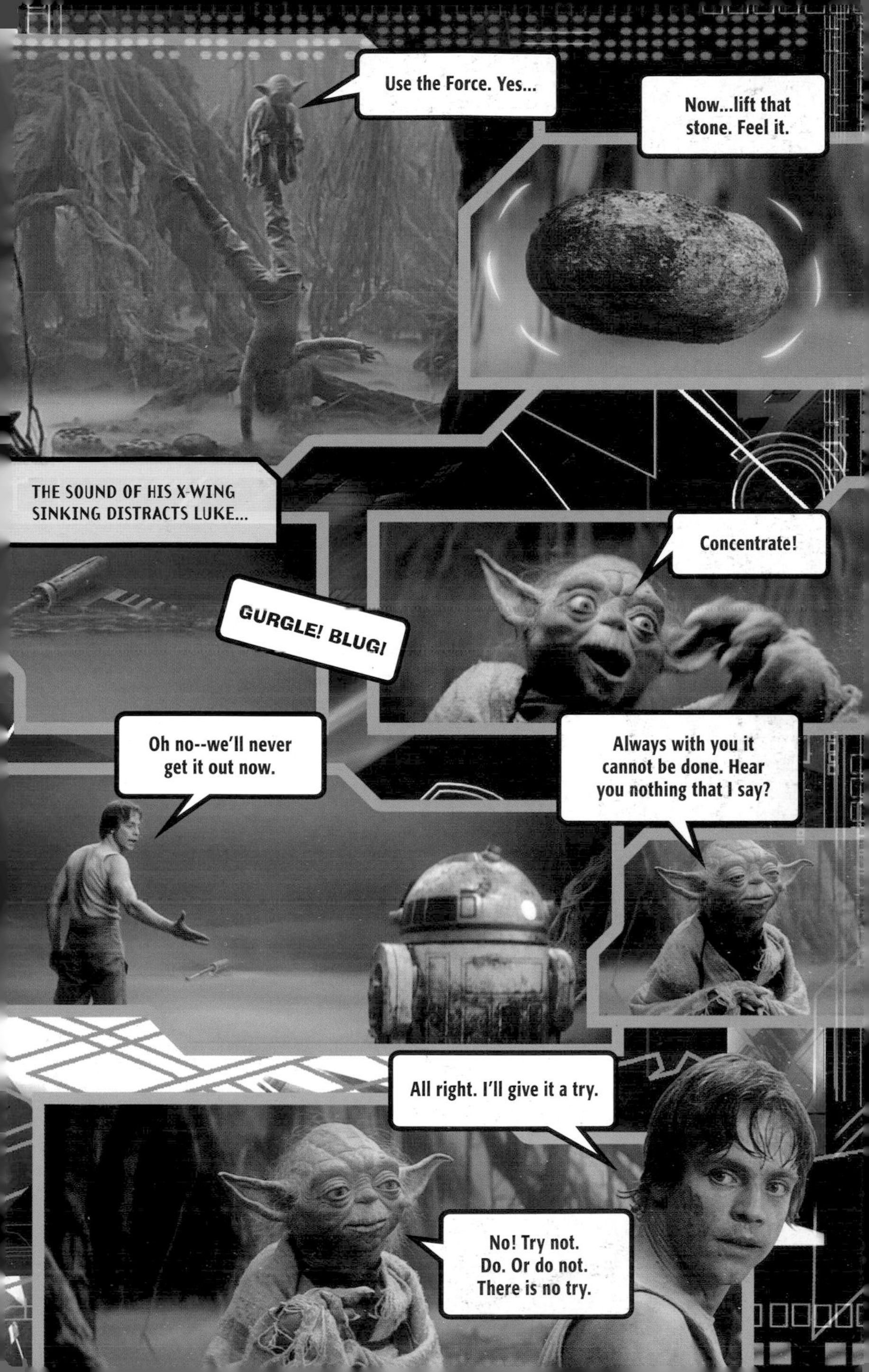
Use the Force. Yes...
Now...lift that stone. Feel it.
THE SOUND OF HIS X-WING SINKING DISTRACTS LUKE...
GURGLE! BLUG!
Concentrate!
Oh no--we'll never get it out now.
Always with you it cannot be done. Hear you nothing that I say?
All right. I'll give it a try.
No! Try not. Do. Or do not. There is no try.

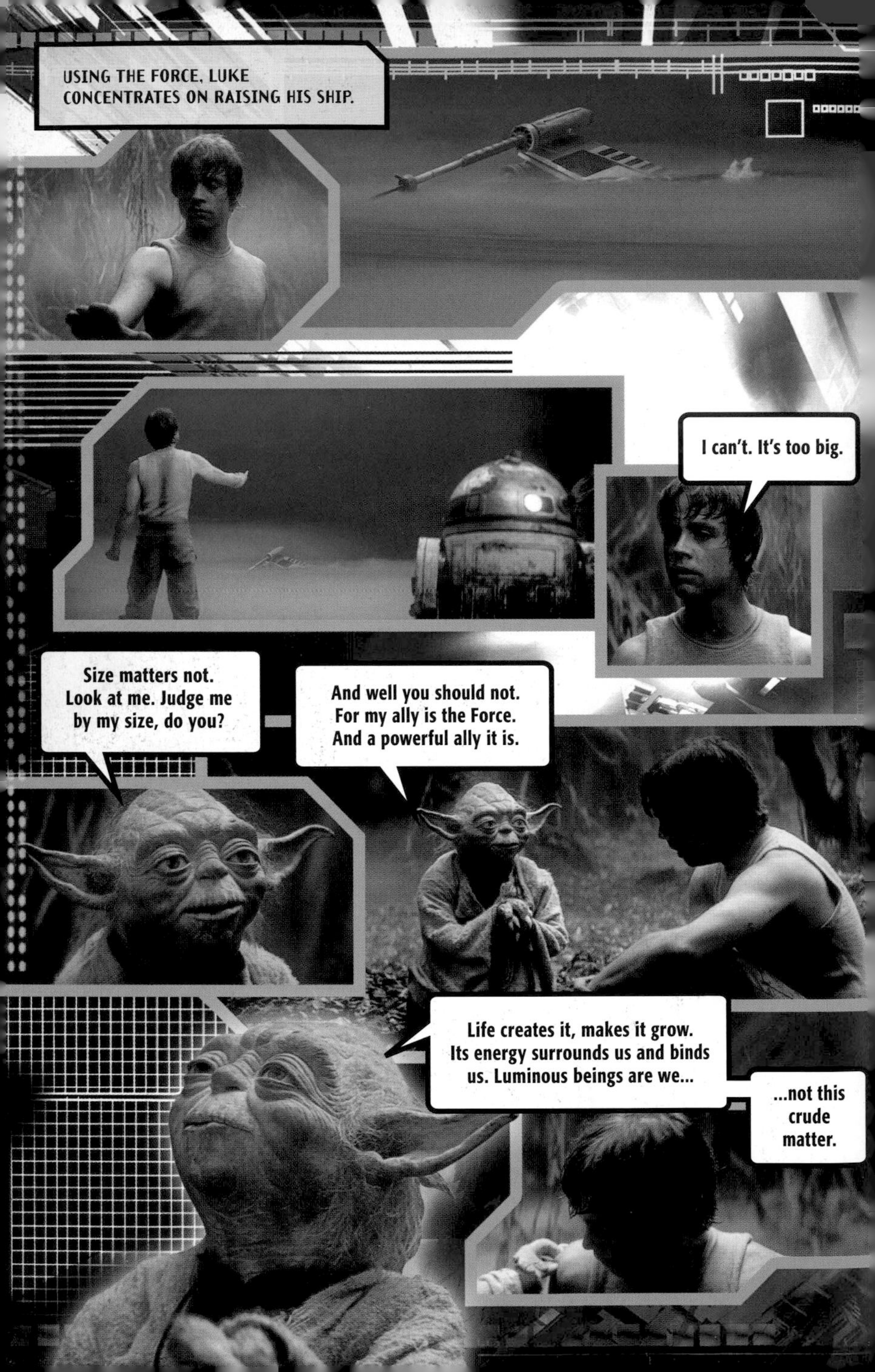
USING THE FORCE, LUKE CONCENTRATES ON RAISING HIS SHIP.
I can't. It's too big.
Size matters not. Look at me. Judge me by my size, do you?
And well you should not. For my ally is the Force. And a powerful ally it is.
Life creates it, makes it grow. Its energy surrounds us and binds us. Luminous beings are we...
...not this crude matter.

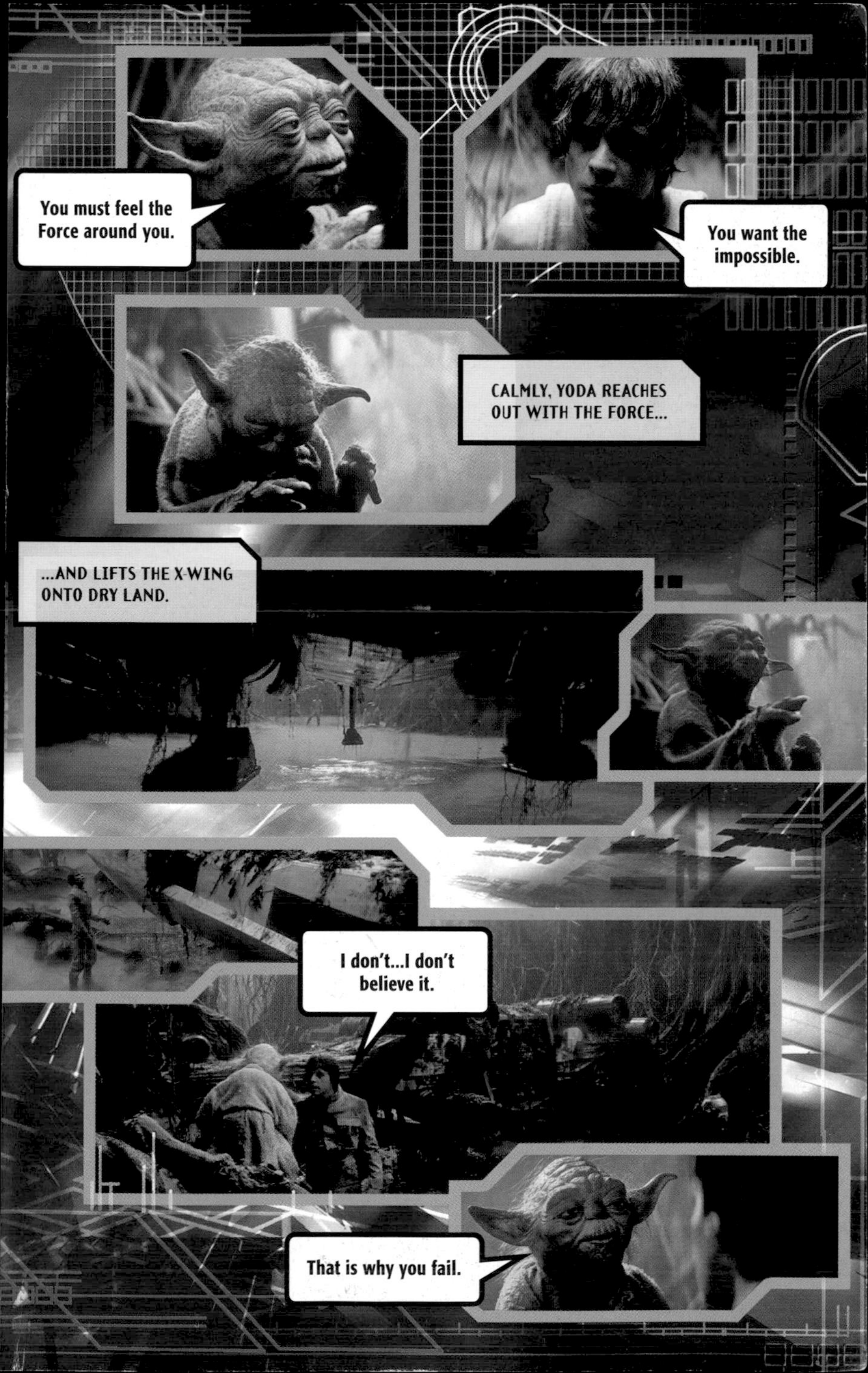
You must feel the Force around you.
You want the impossible.
CALMLY, YODA REACHES OUT WITH THE FORCE...
...AND LIFTS THE X-WING ONTO DRY LAND.
I don't...I don't believe it.
That is why you fail.

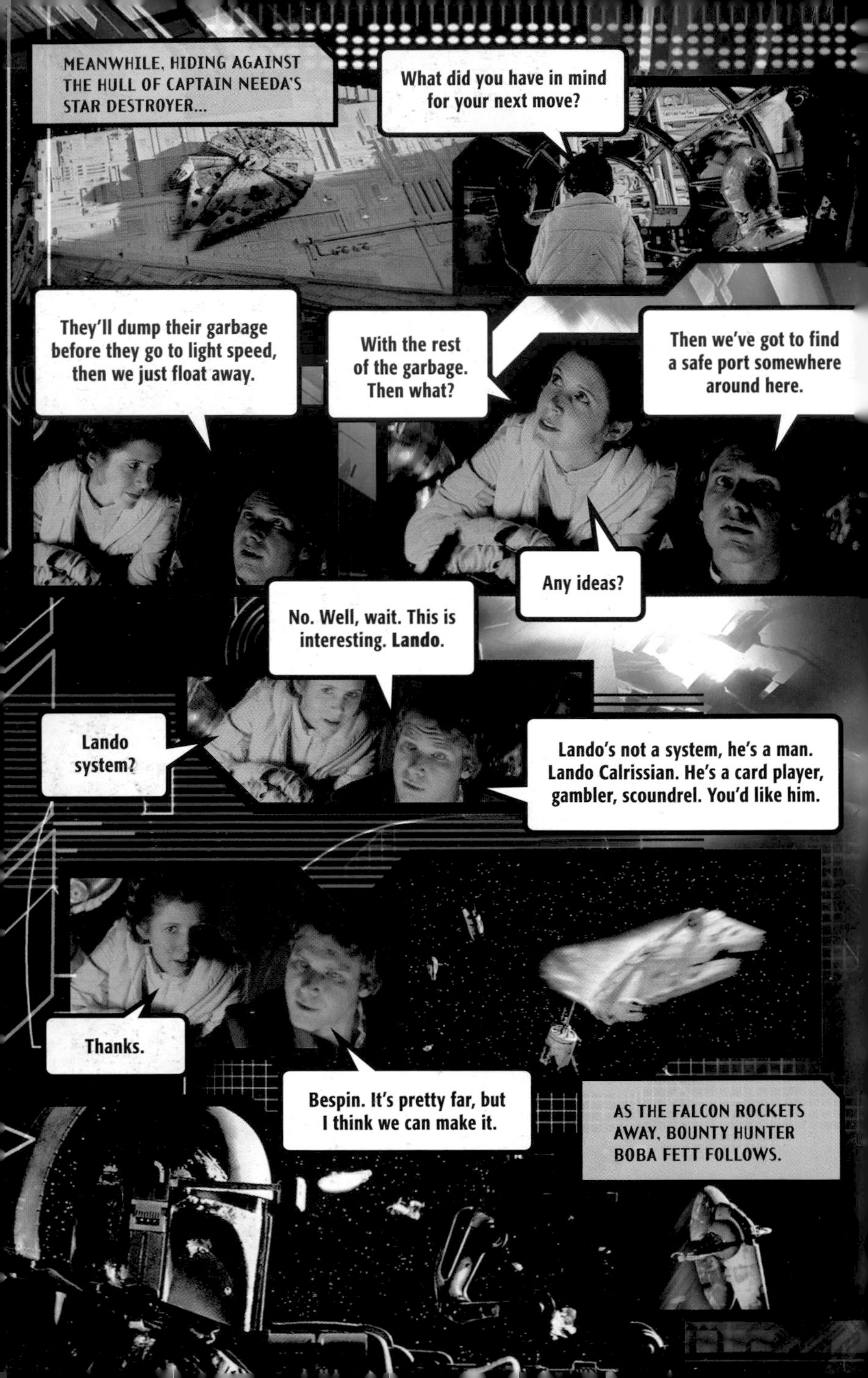
MEANWHILE, HIDING AGAINST THE HULL OF CAPTAIN NEEDA'S STAR DESTROYER...
What did you have in mind for your next move?
They'll dump their garbage before they go to light speed, then we just float away.
With the rest of the garbage. Then what?
Then we've got to find a safe port somewhere around here.
Any ideas?
No. Well, wait. This is interesting. Lando.
Lando system?
Lando's not a system, he's a man. Lando Calrissian. He's a card player, gambler, scoundrel. You'd like him.
Thanks.
Bespin. It's pretty far, but I think we can make it.
AS THE FALCON ROCKETS AWAY, BOUNTY HUNTER BOBA FETT FOLLOWS.

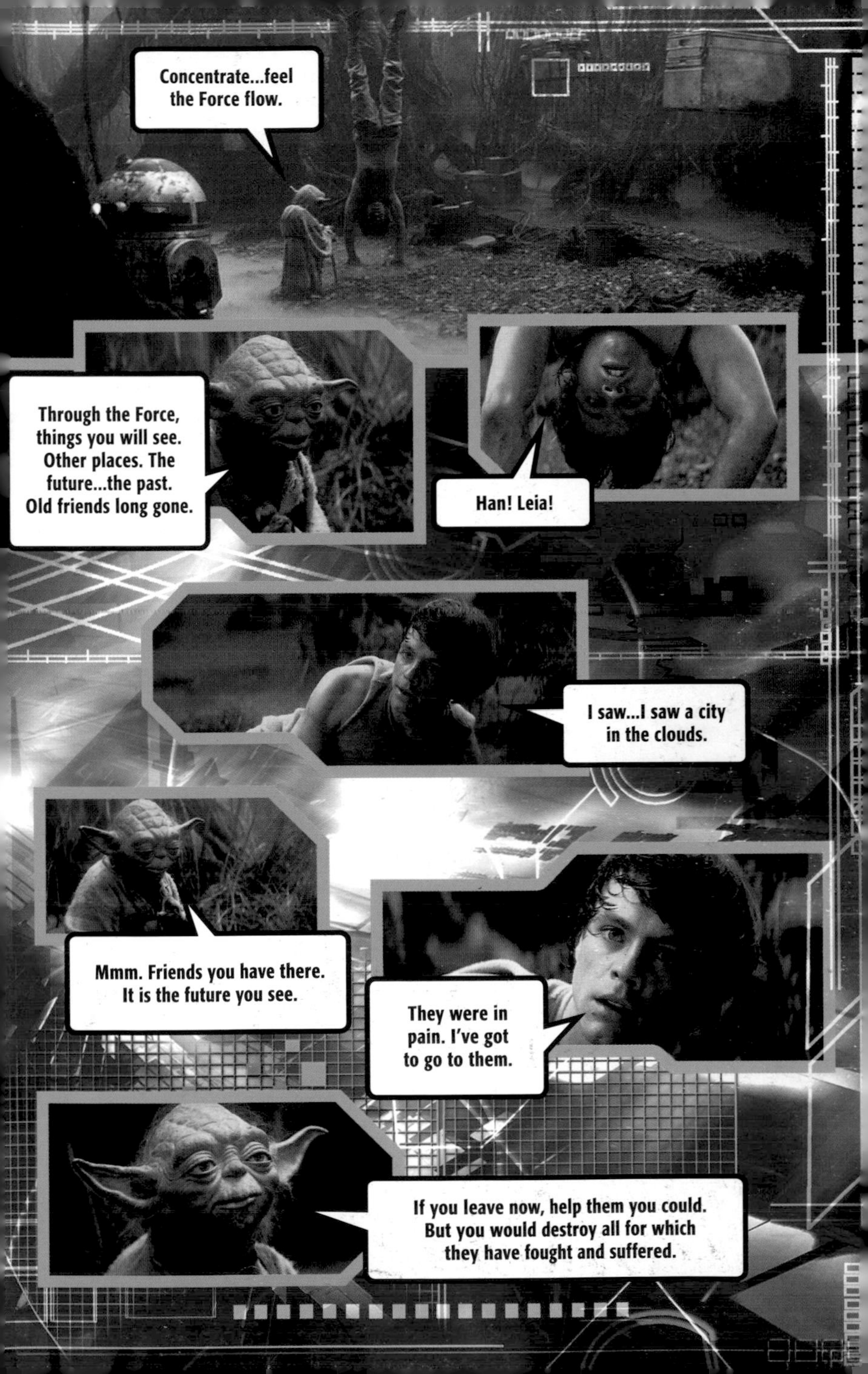

Concentrate...feel the Force flow.
Through the Force, things you will see. Other places. The future...the past. Old friends long gone.
Han! Leia!
I saw...I saw a city in the clouds.
Mmm. Friends you have there. It is the future you see.
They were in pain. I've got to go to them.
If you leave now, help them you could. But you would destroy all for which they have fought and suffered.

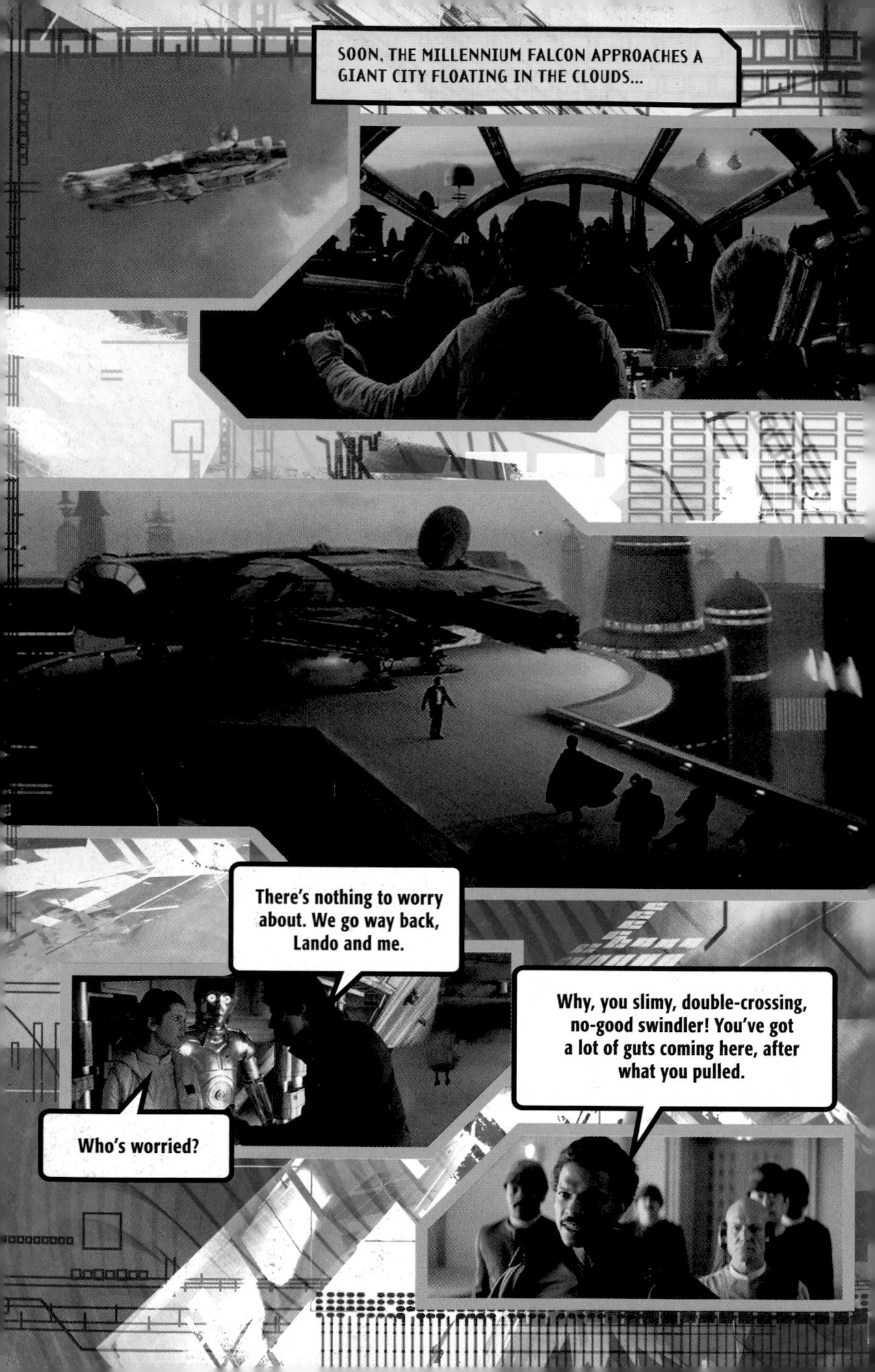
SOON, THE MILLENNIUM FALCON APPROACHES A GIANT CITY FLOATING IN THE CLOUDS...
There's nothing to worry about. We go way back, Lando and me.
Who's worried?
Why, you slimy, double-crossing, no-good swindler! You've got a lot of guts coming here, after what you pulled.

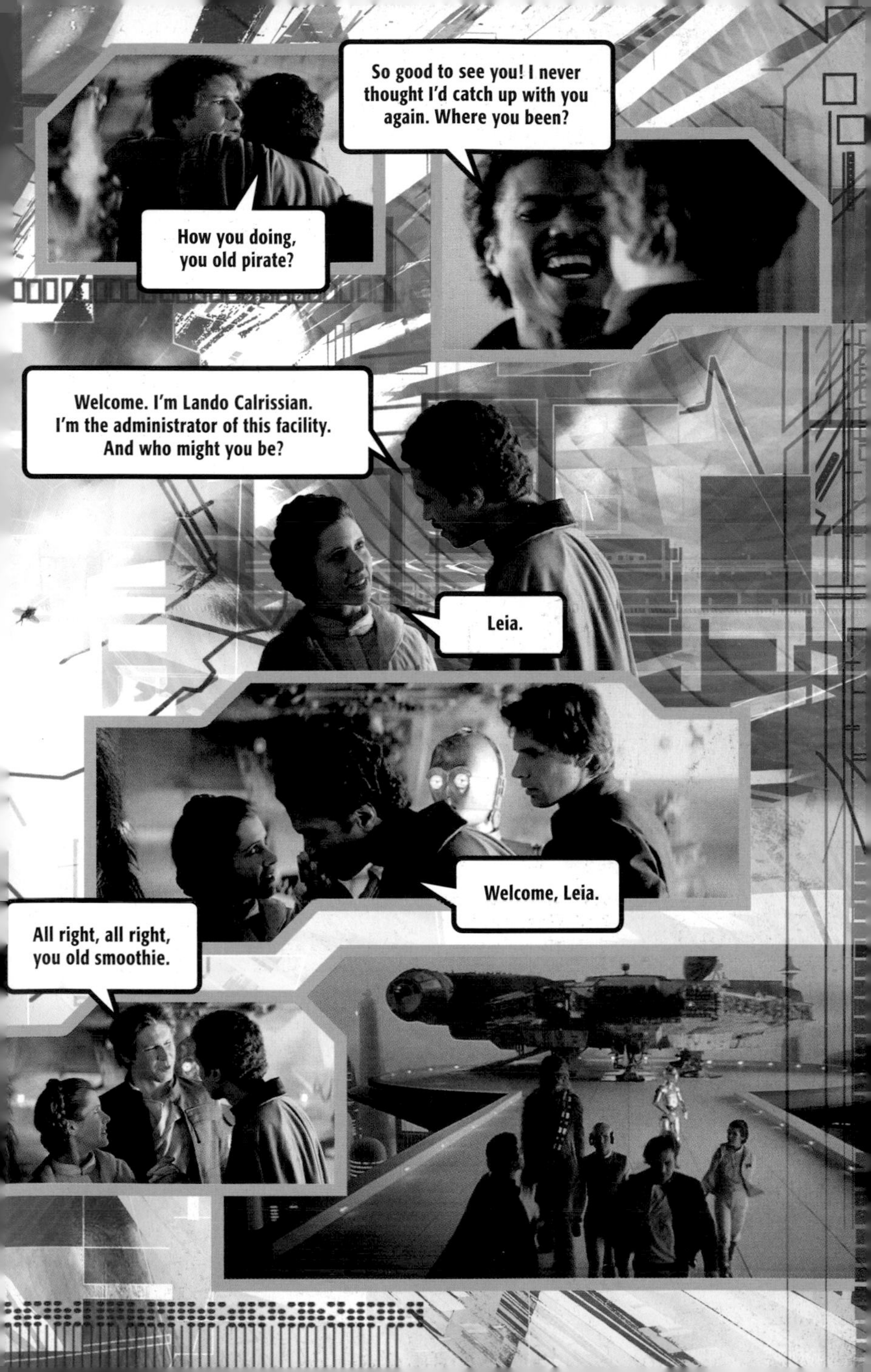
How you doing,
you old pirate?
So good to see you! I never thought I'd catch up with you again. Where you been?
Welcome. I'm Lando Calrissian. I'm the administrator of this facility. And who might you be?
Leia.
Welcome, Leia.
All right, all right, you old smoothie.

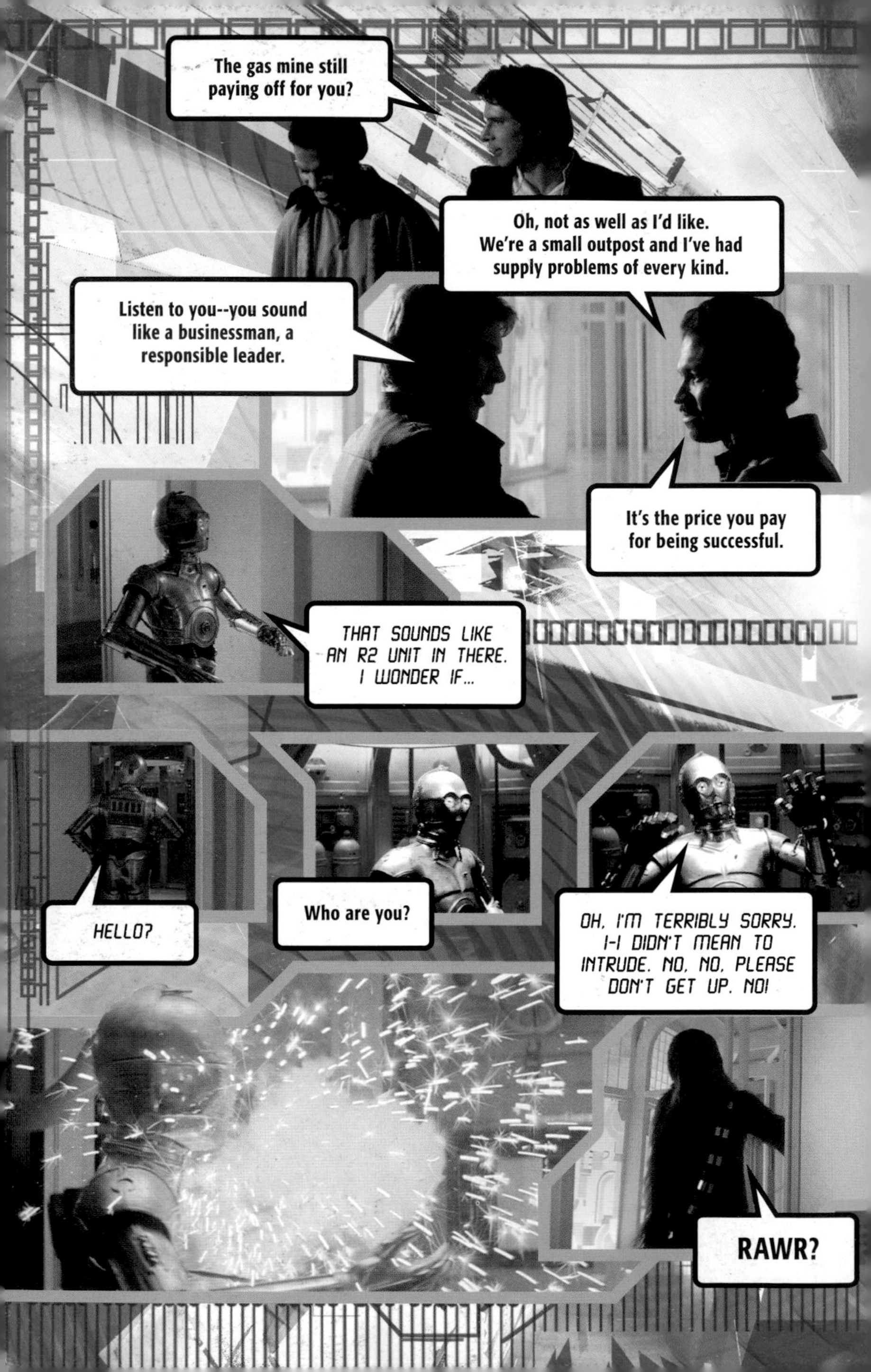

The gas mine still paying off for you?
Oh, not as well as I'd like. We're a small outpost and I've had supply problems of every kind.
Listen to you--you sound like a businessman, a responsible leader.
It's the price you pay for being successful.
THAT SOUNDS LIKE AN R2 UNIT IN THERE. I WONDER IF...
HELLO?
Who are you?
OH, I'M TERRIBLY SORRY. I-I DIDN'T MEAN TO INTRUDE. NO, NO, PLEASE DON'T GET UP. NO!
RAWR?

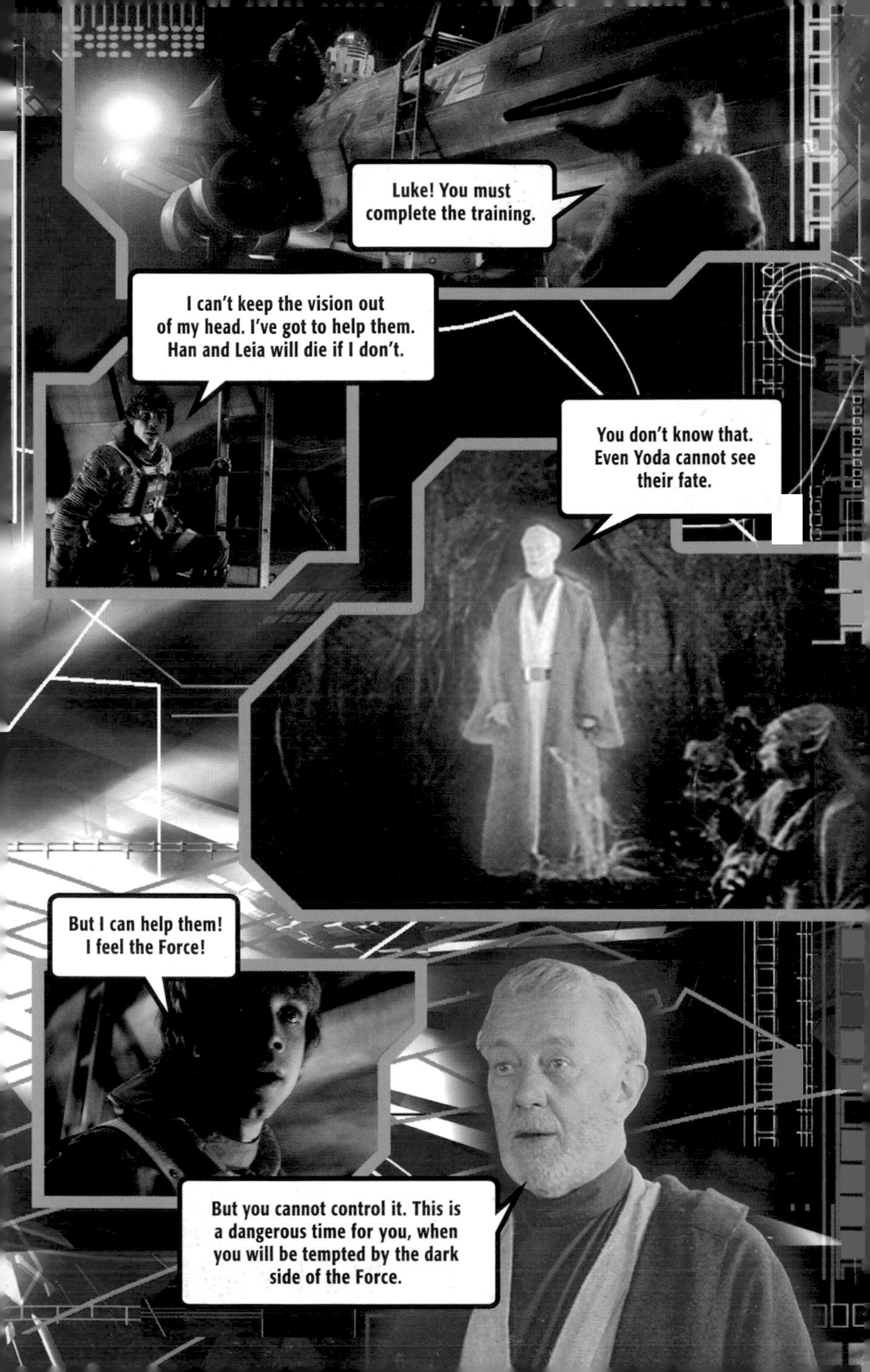
Luke! You must complete the training.
I can't keep the vision out of my head. I've got to help them. Han and Leia will die if I don't.
You don't know that. Even Yoda cannot see their fate.
But I can help them! I feel the Force!
But you cannot control it. This is a dangerous time for you, when you will be tempted by the dark side of the Force.

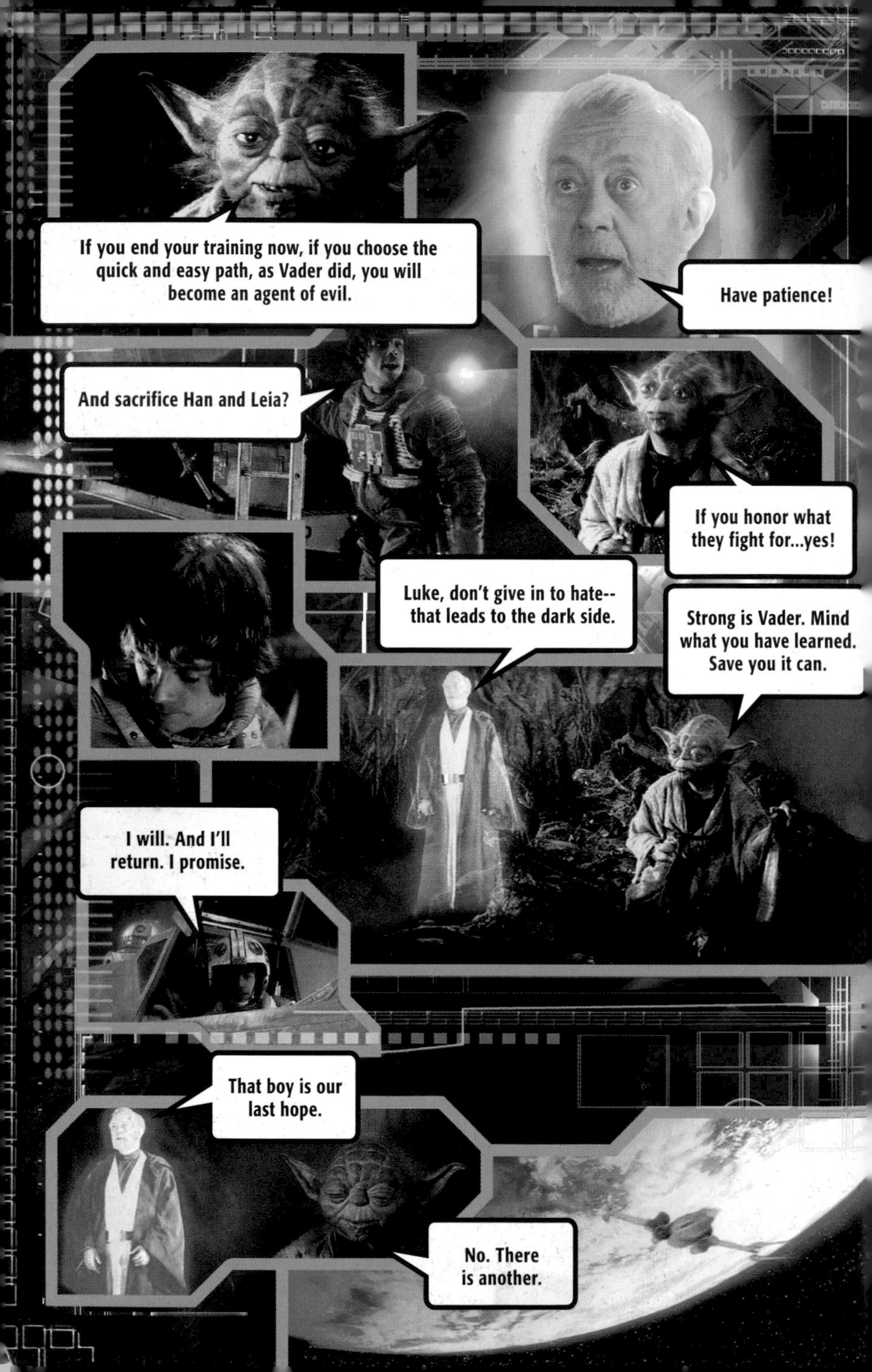
If you end your training now, if you choose the quick and easy path, as Vader did, you will become an agent of evil.
Have patience!
And sacrifice Han and Leia?
If you honor what they fight for...yes!
Luke, don't give in to hate--that leads to the dark side.
Strong is Vader. Mind what you have learned. Save you it can.
I will. And I'll return. I promise.
That boy is our last hope.
No. There is another.

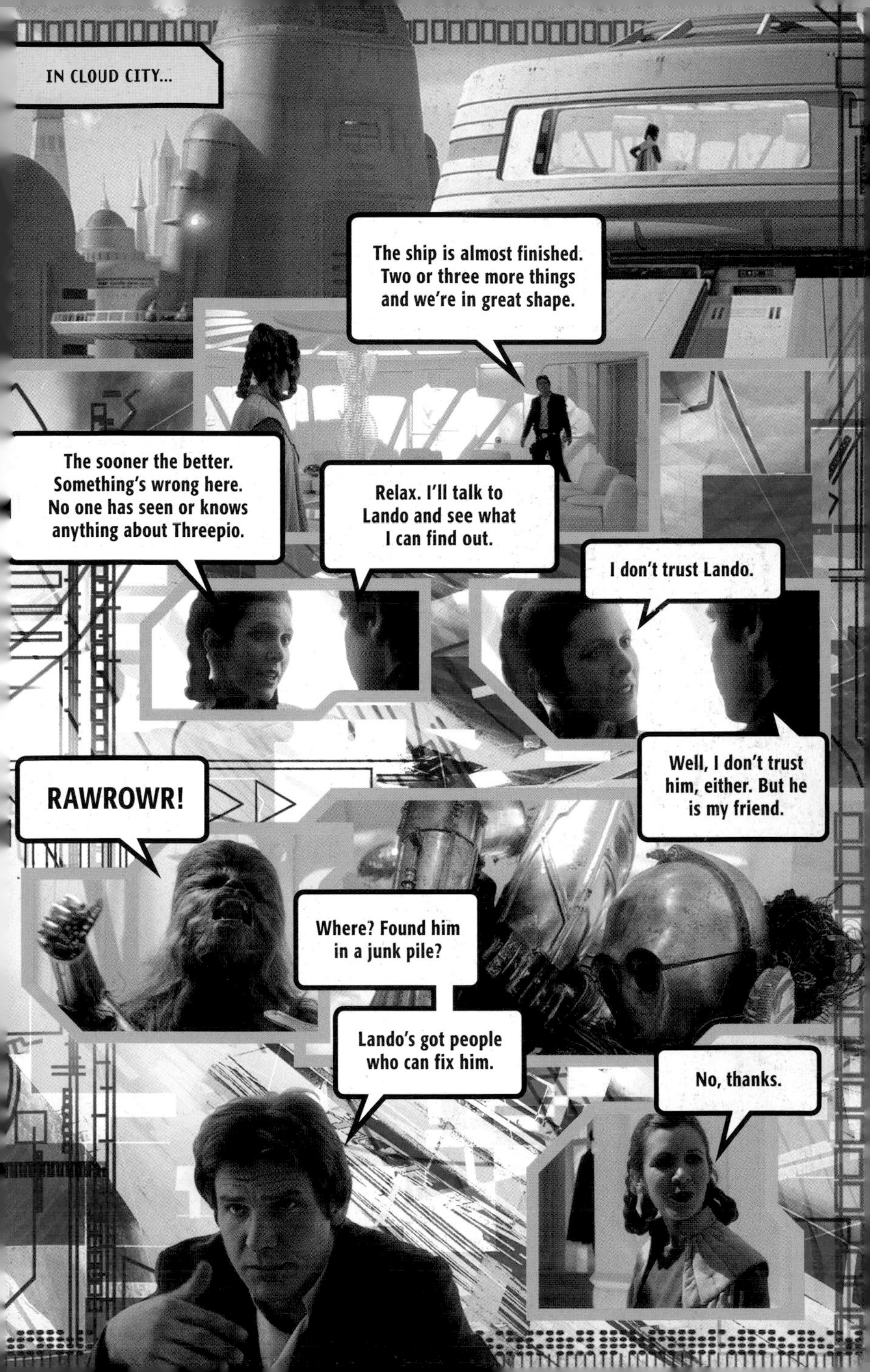
IN CLOUD CITY...
The ship is almost finished. Two or three more things and we're in great shape.
The sooner the better. Something's wrong here. No one has seen or knows anything about Threepio.
Relax. I'll talk to Lando and see what I can find out.
I don't trust Lando.
Well, I don't trust him, either. But he is my friend.
RAWROWR!
Where? Found him in a junk pile?
Lando's got people who can fix him.
No, thanks.

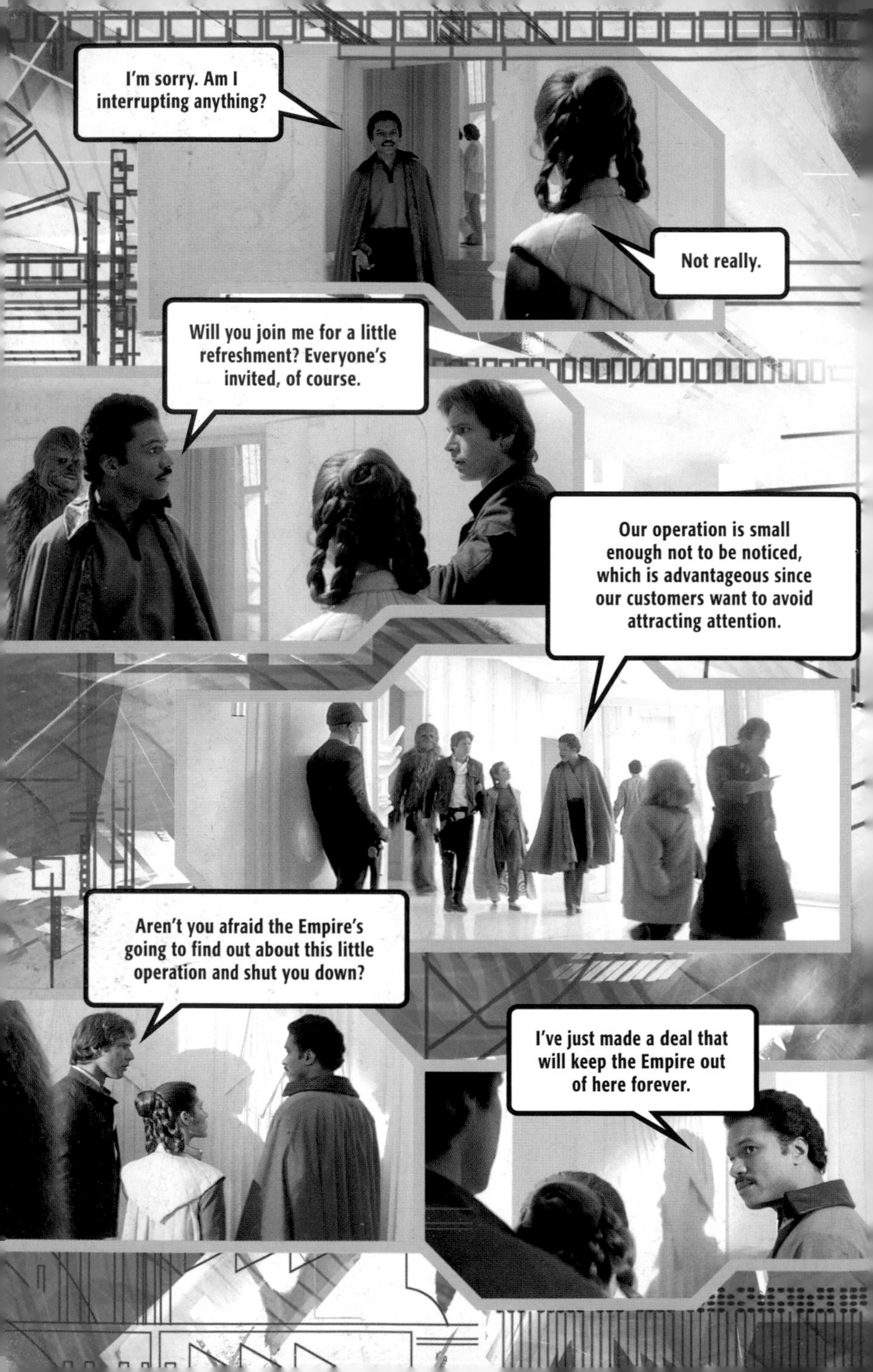
I'm sorry. Am I interrupting anything?
Not really.
Will you join me for a little refreshment? Everyone's invited, of course.
Our operation is small enough not to be noticed, which is advantageous since our customers want to avoid attracting attention.
Aren't you afraid the Empire's going to find out about this little operation and shut you down?
I've just made a deal that will keep the Empire out of here forever.

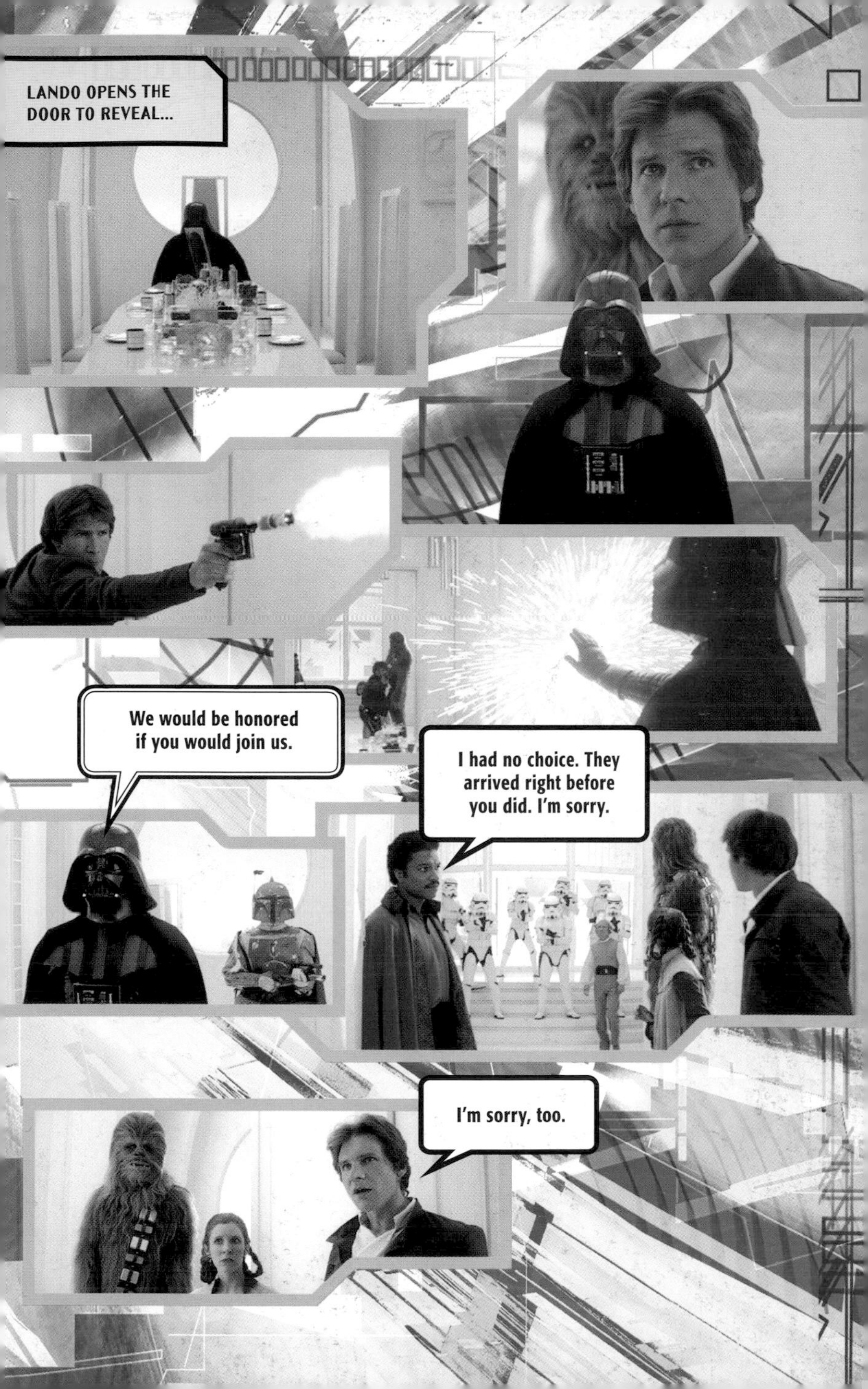
LANDO OPENS THE DOOR TO REVEAL...
We would be honored if you would join us.
I had no choice. They arrived right before you did. I'm sorry.
I'm sorry, too.

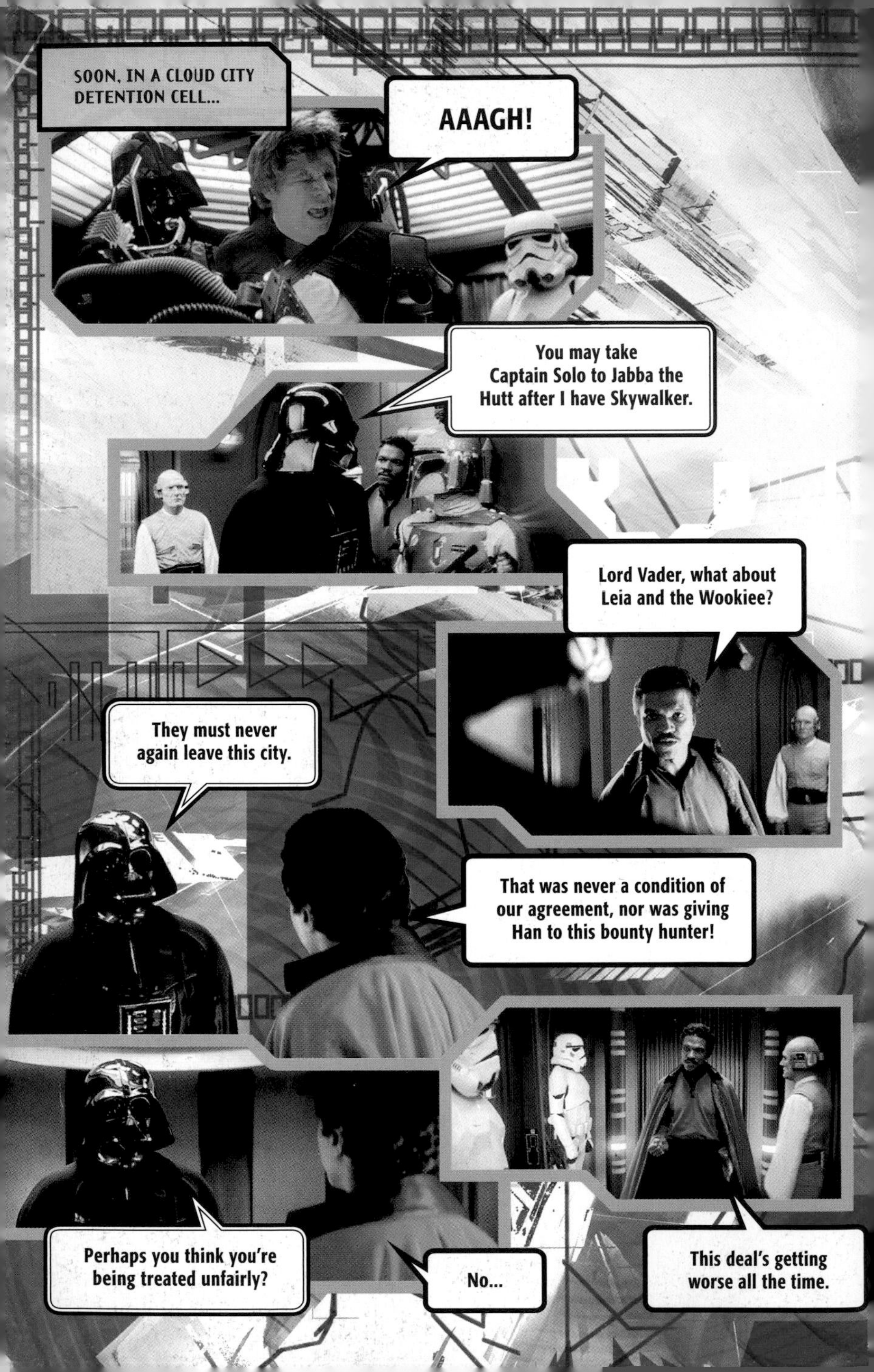
SOON, IN A CLOUD CITY DETENTION CELL...
AAAGH!
You may take Captain Solo to Jabba the Hutt after I have Skywalker.
Lord Vader, what about Leia and the Wookiee?
They must never again leave this city.
That was never a condition of our agreement, nor was giving Han to this bounty hunter!
Perhaps you think you're being treated unfairly?
No...
This deal's getting worse all the time.

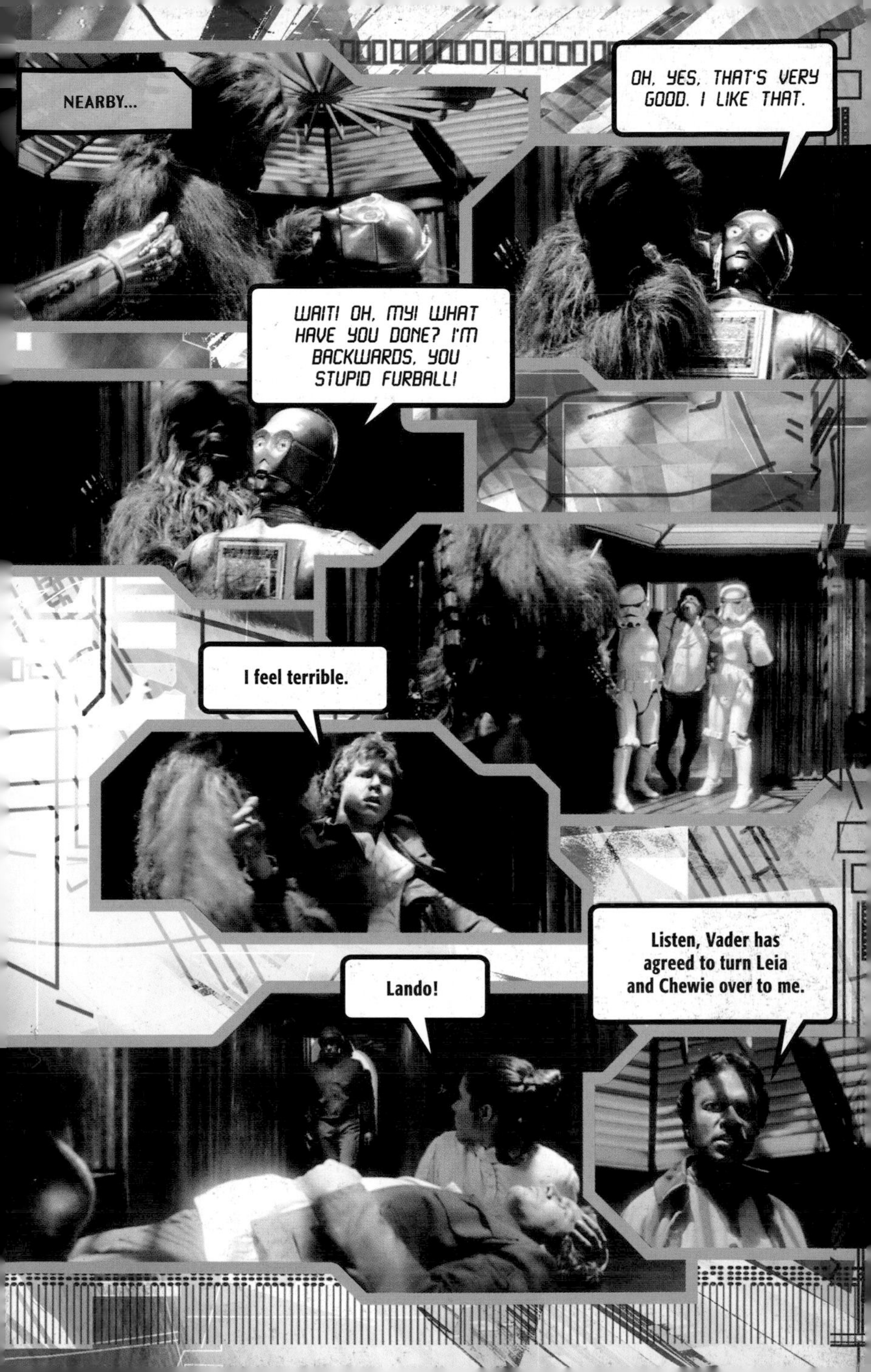
NEARBY...
OH, YES, THAT'S VERY GOOD. I LIKE THAT.
WAIT! OH, MY! WHAT HAVE YOU DONE? I'M BACKWARDS, YOU STUPID FURBALL!
I feel terrible.
Listen, Vader has agreed to turn Leia and Chewie over to me.
Lando!

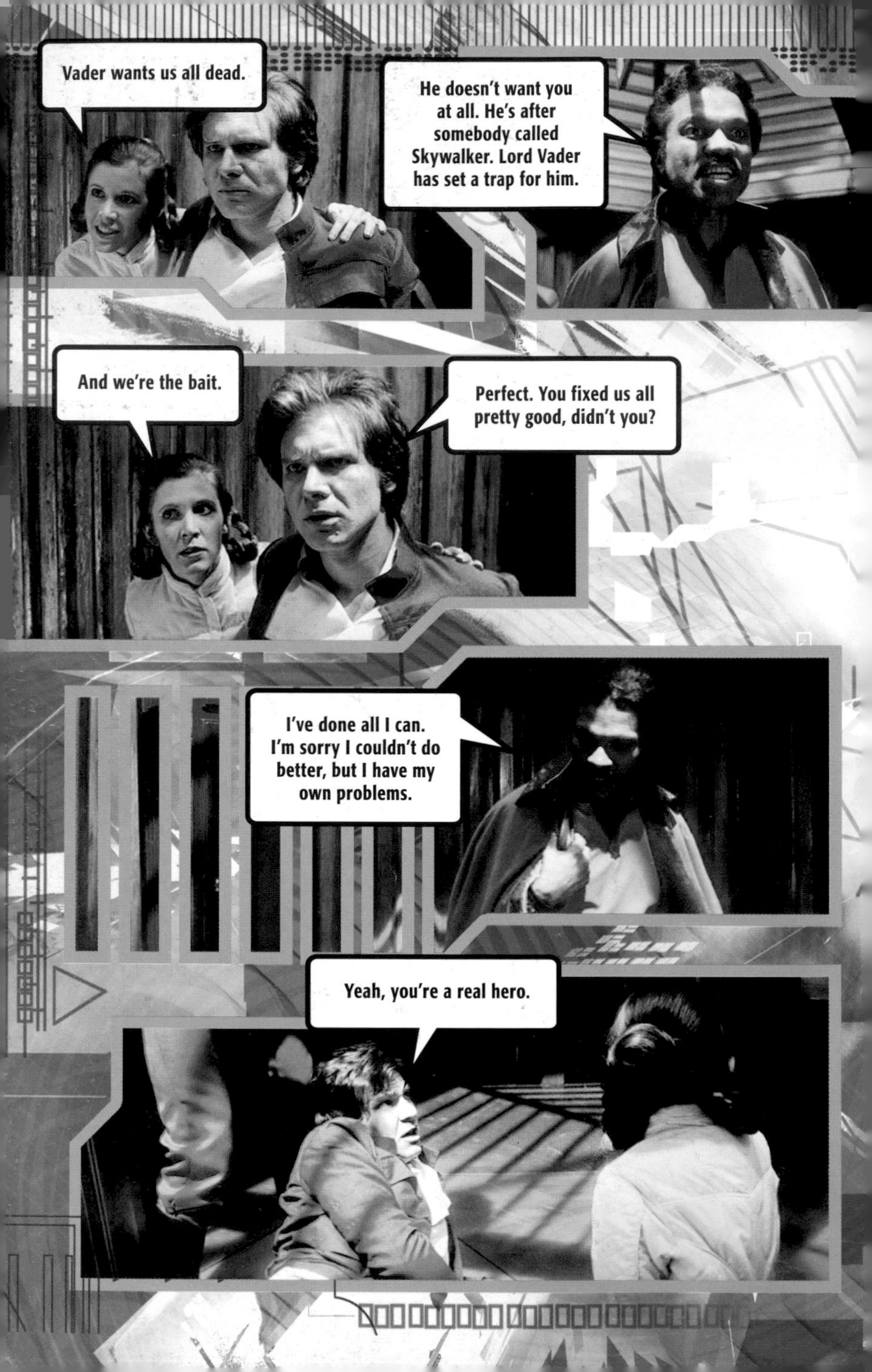
Vader wants us all dead.
He doesn't want you at all. He's after somebody called Skywalker. Lord Vader has set a trap for him.
And we're the bait.
Perfect. You fixed us all pretty good, didn't you?
I've done all I can. I'm sorry I couldn't do better, but I have my own problems.
Yeah, you're a real hero.

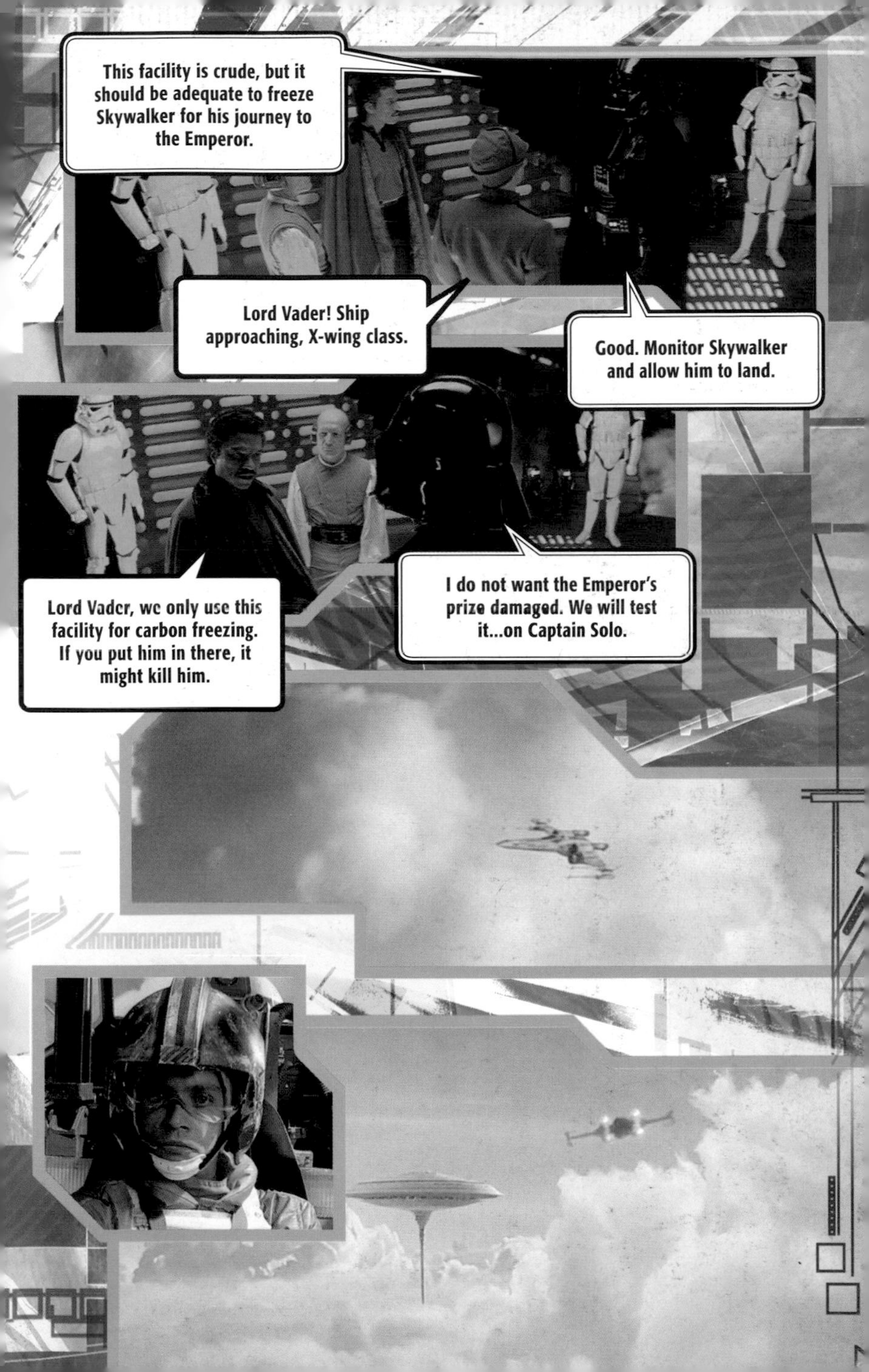
This facility is crude, but it should be adequate to freeze Skywalker for his journey to the Emperor.
Lord Vader! Ship approaching, X-wing class.
Good. Monitor Skywalker and allow him to land.
Lord Vader, we only use this facility for carbon freezing. If you put him in there, it might kill him.
I do not want the Emperor's prize damaged. We will test it...on Captain Solo.

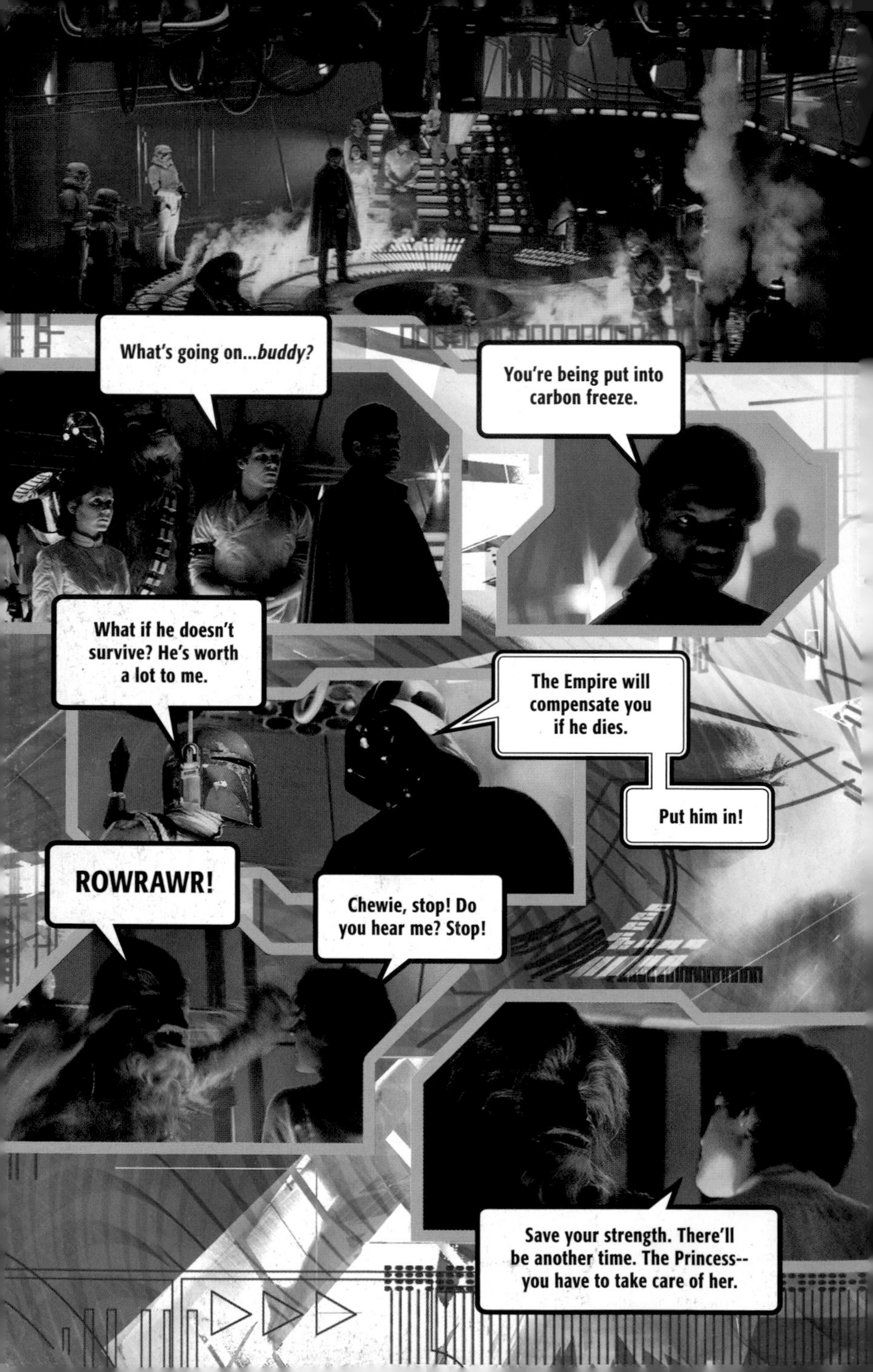
What's going on...*buddy?*
You're being put into carbon freeze.
What if he doesn't survive? He's worth a lot to me.
The Empire will compensate you if he dies.
Put him in!
ROWRAWR!
Chewie, stop! Do you hear me? Stop!
Save your strength. There'll be another time. The Princess--you have to take care of her.

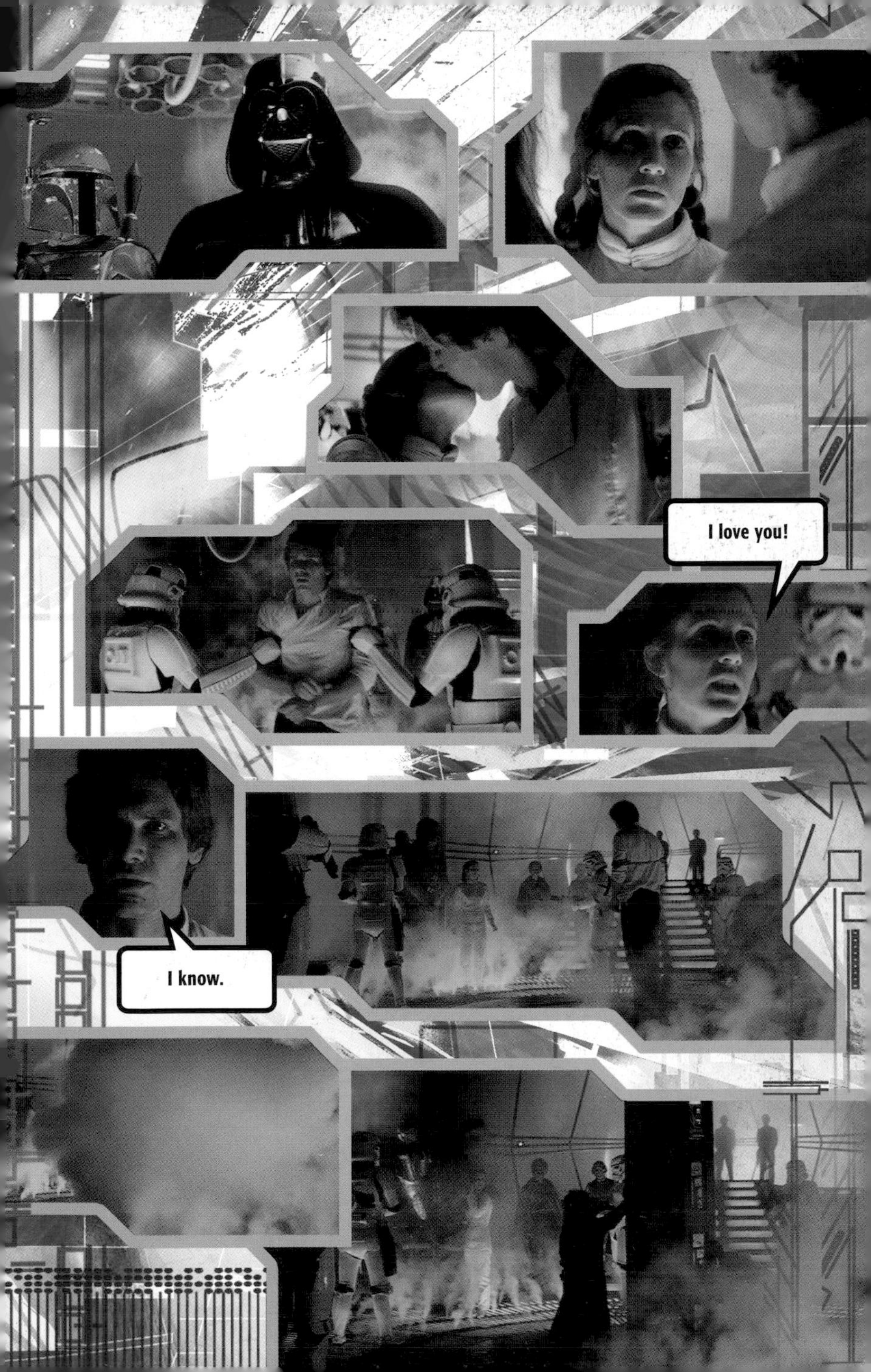
I love you!
I know.

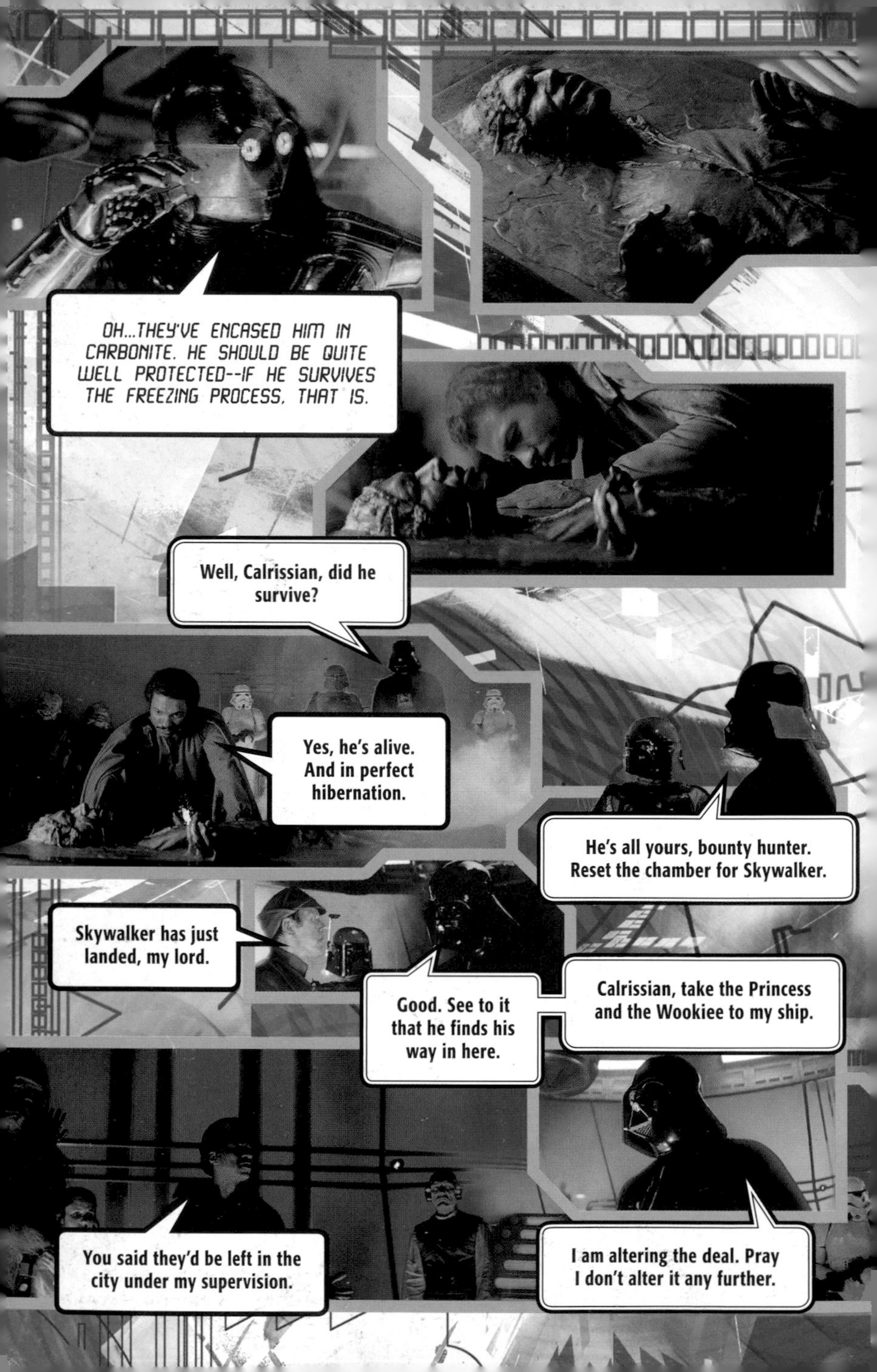

OH...THEY'VE ENCASED HIM IN CARBONITE. HE SHOULD BE QUITE WELL PROTECTED--IF HE SURVIVES THE FREEZING PROCESS, THAT IS.
Well, Calrissian, did he survive?
Yes, he's alive. And in perfect hibernation.
He's all yours, bounty hunter. Reset the chamber for Skywalker.
Skywalker has just landed, my lord.
Good. See to it that he finds his way in here.
Calrissian, take the Princess and the Wookiee to my ship.
You said they'd be left in the city under my supervision.
I am altering the deal. Pray I don't alter it any further.

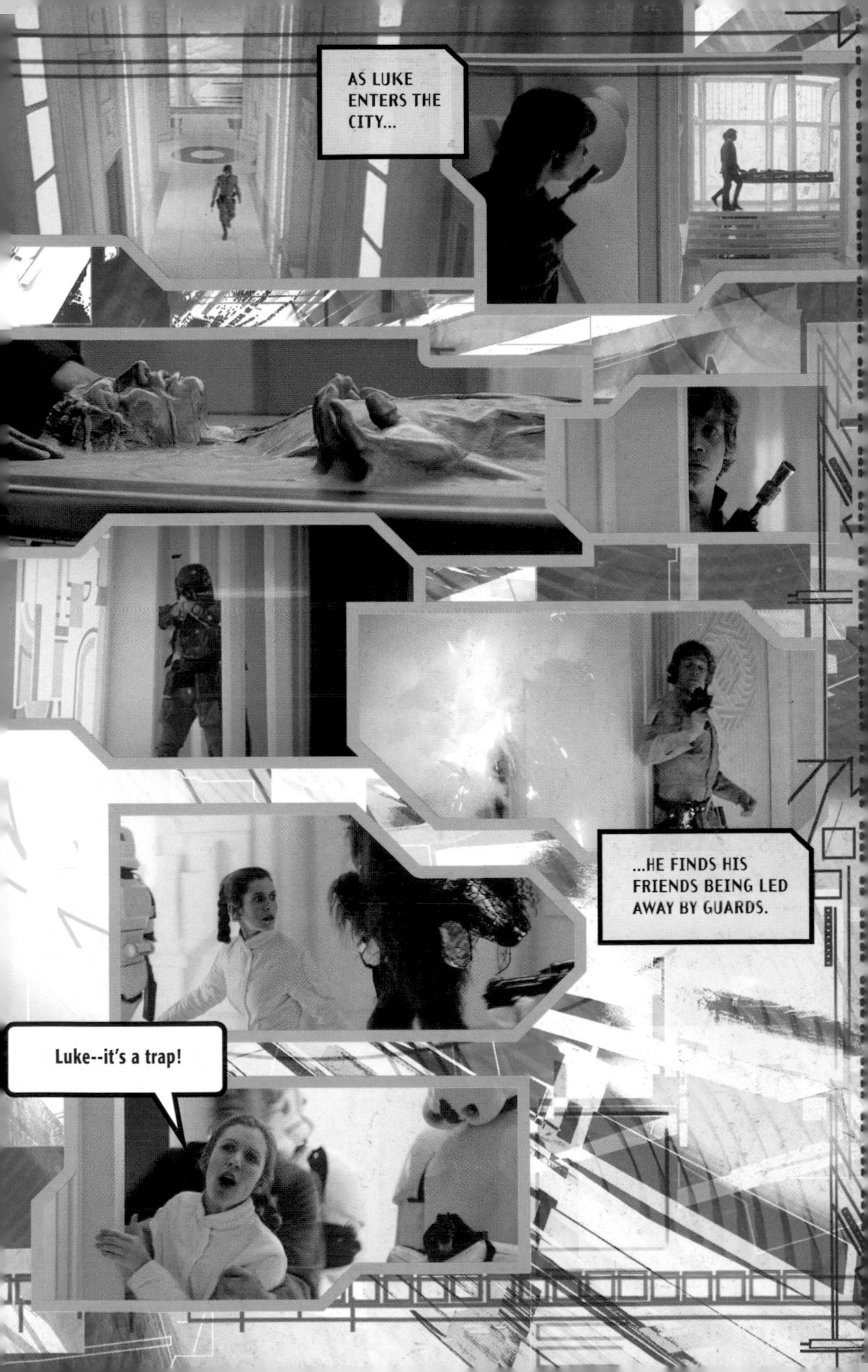
AS LUKE ENTERS THE CITY...
...HE FINDS HIS FRIENDS BEING LED AWAY BY GUARDS.
Luke--it's a trap!

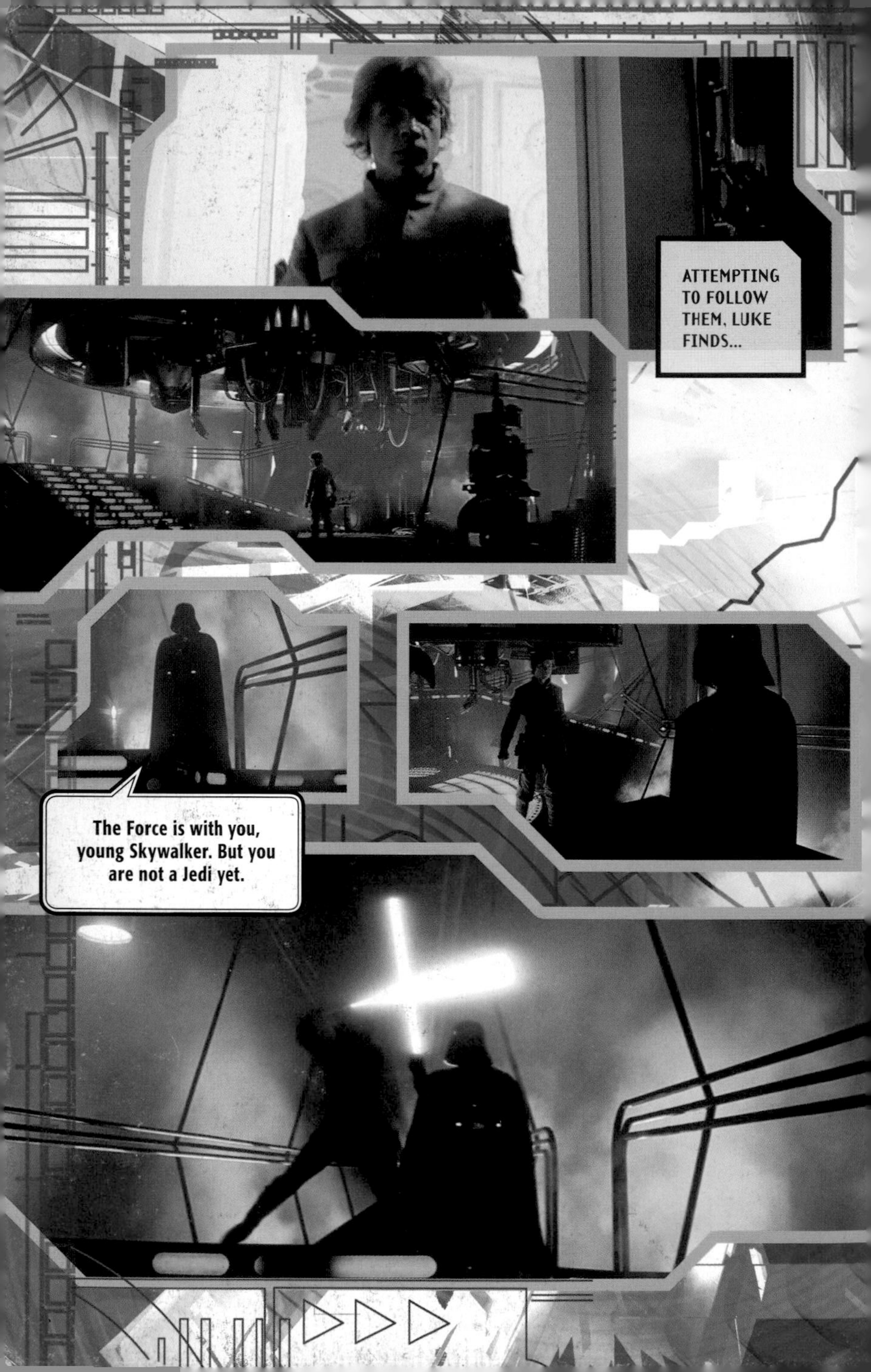
ATTEMPTING TO FOLLOW THEM, LUKE FINDS...
The Force is with you, young Skywalker. But you are not a Jedi yet.

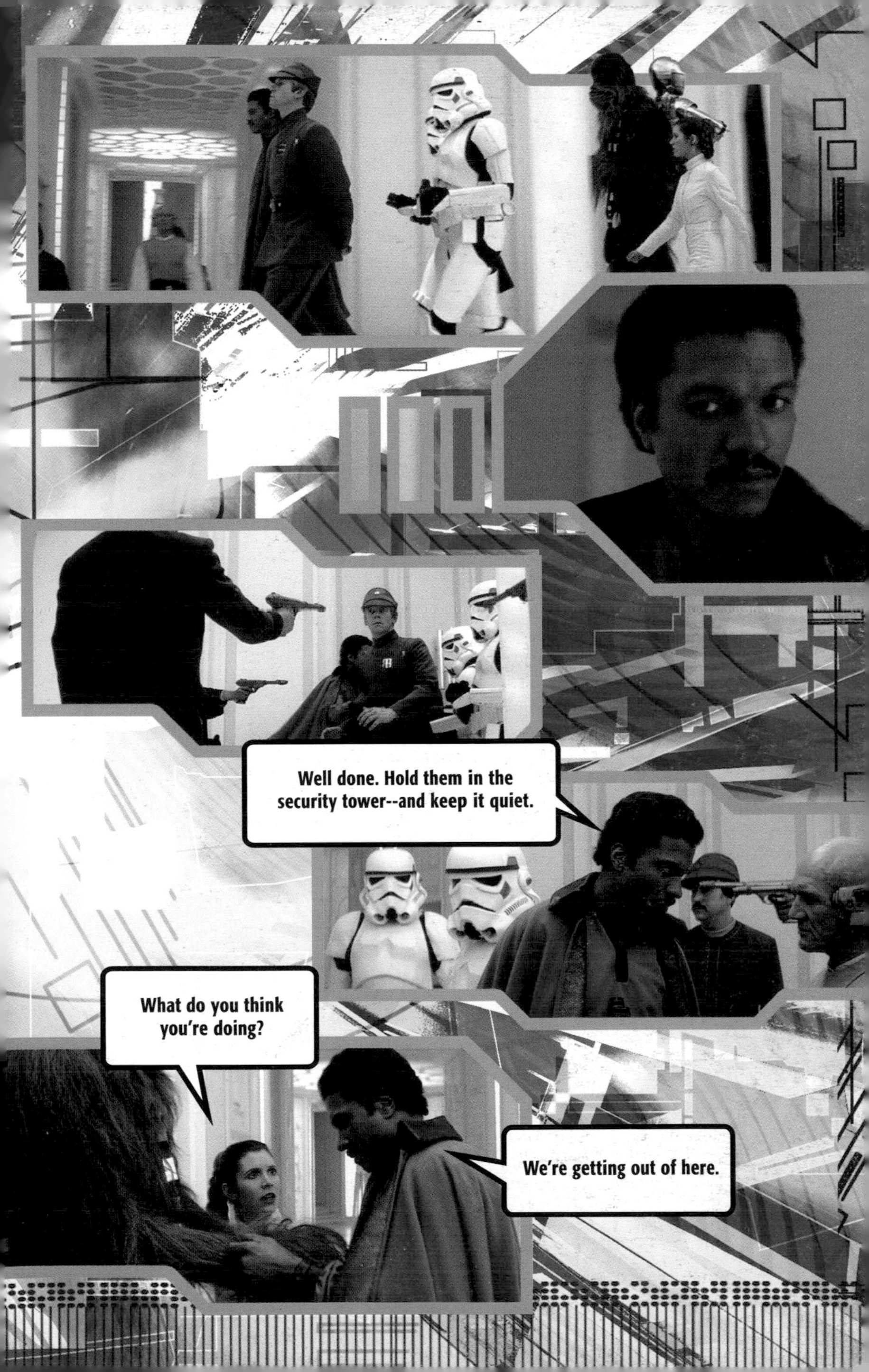
Well done. Hold them in the security tower--and keep it quiet.
What do you think you're doing?
We're getting out of here.

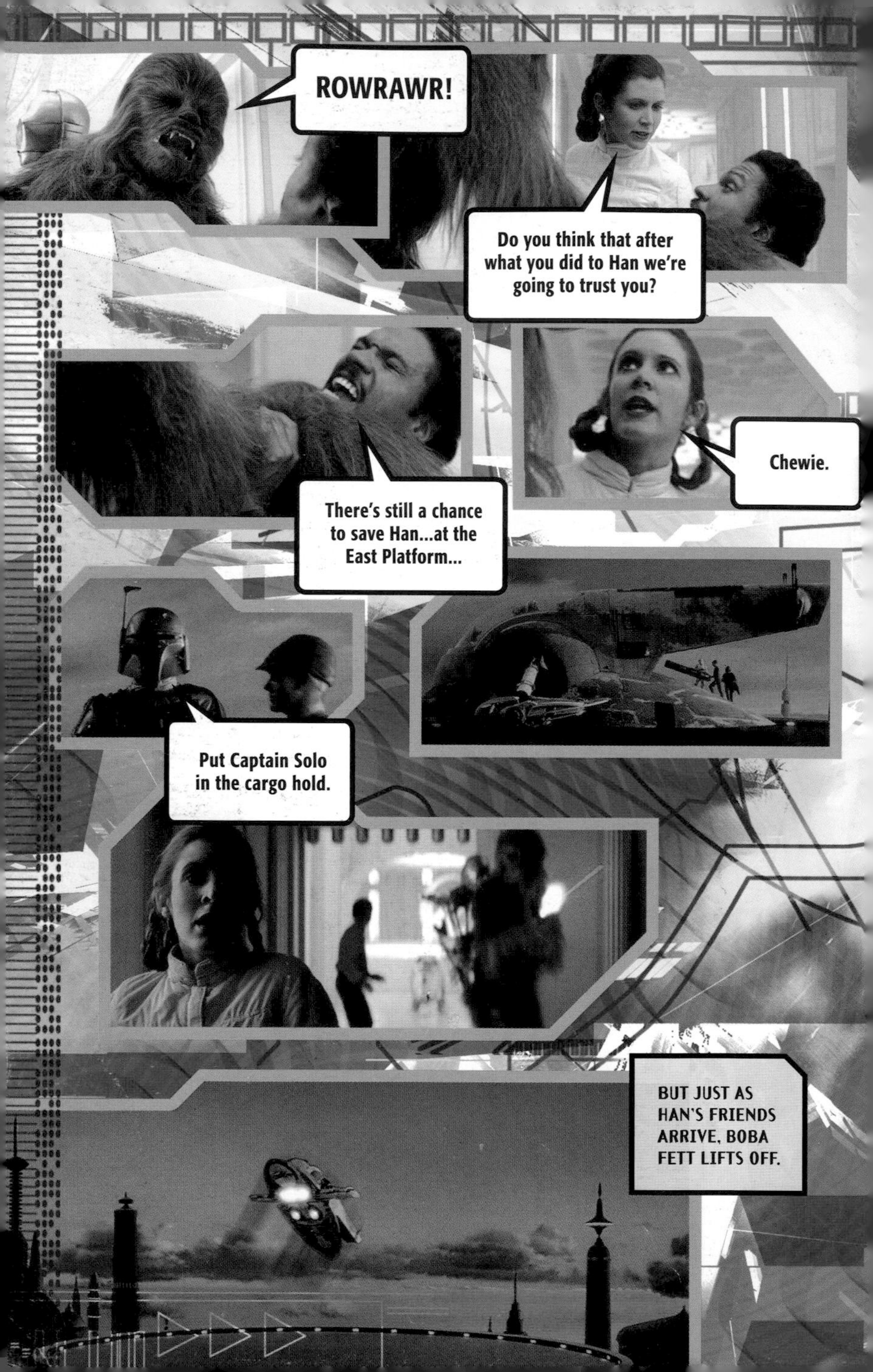
ROWRAWR!
Do you think that after what you did to Han we're going to trust you?
There's still a chance to save Han...at the East Platform...
Chewie.
Put Captain Solo in the cargo hold.
BUT JUST AS HAN'S FRIENDS ARRIVE, BOBA FETT LIFTS OFF.

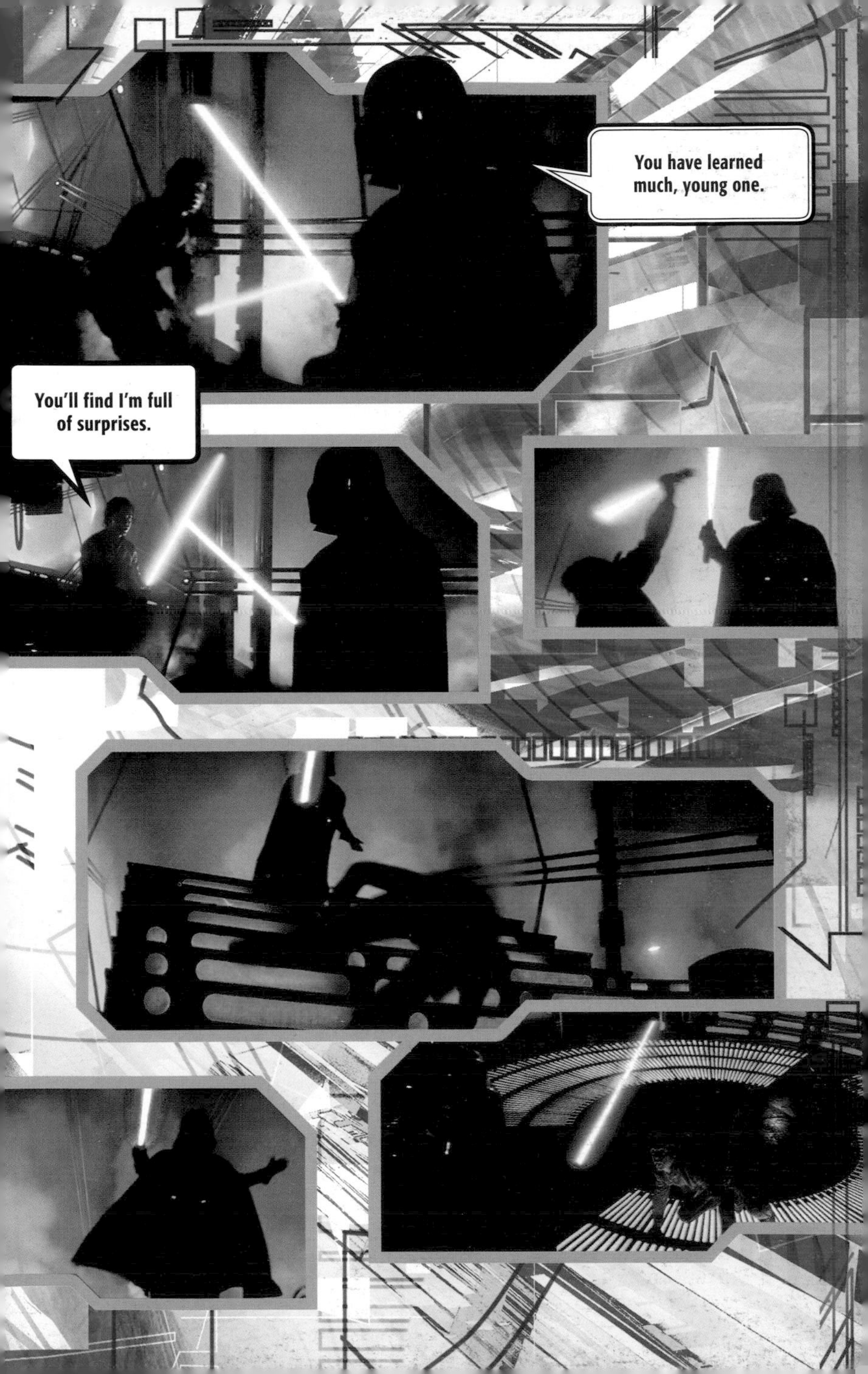
You have learned much, young one.
You'll find I'm full of surprises.

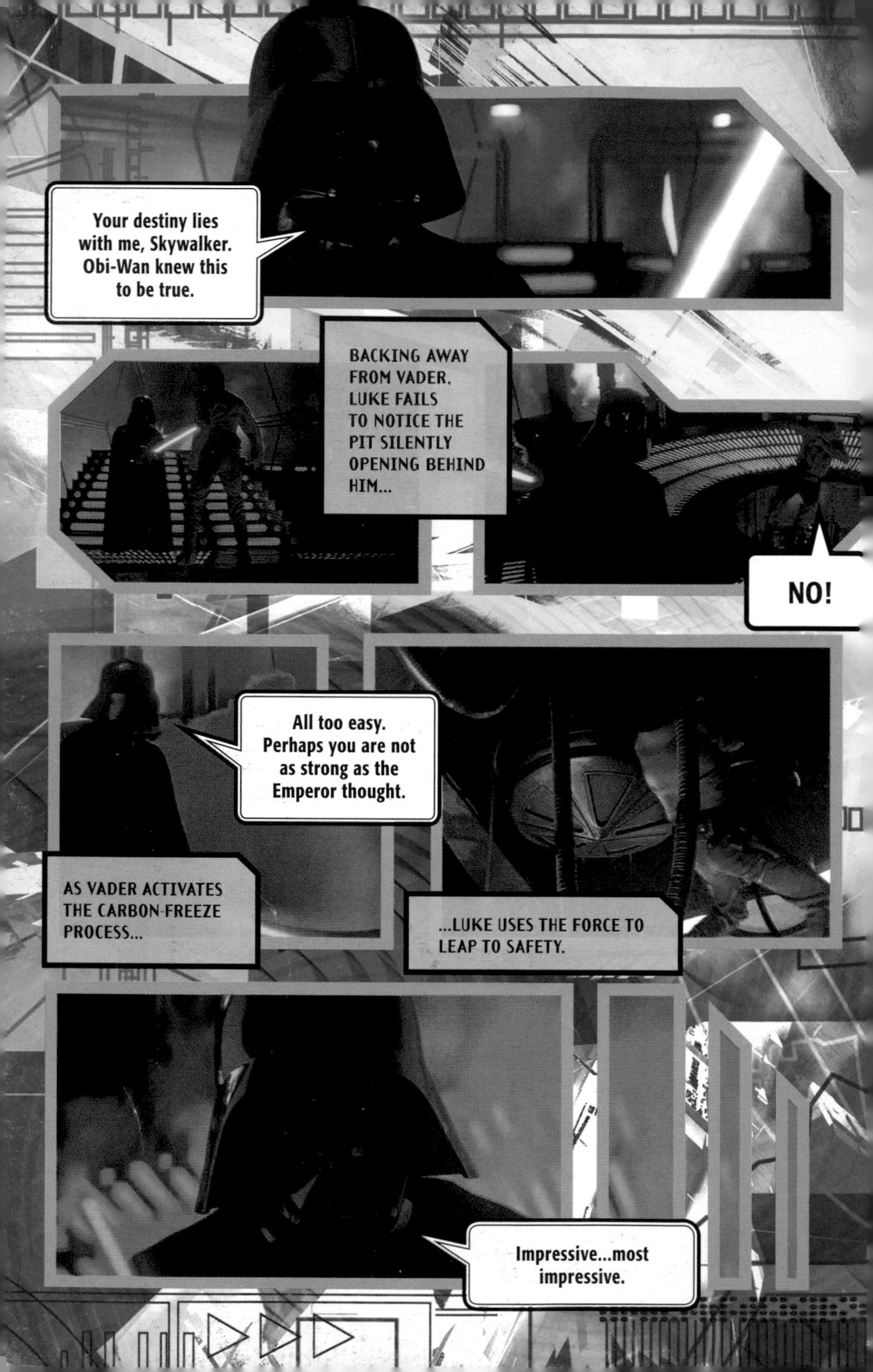
Your destiny lies with me, Skywalker. Obi-Wan knew this to be true.
BACKING AWAY FROM VADER, LUKE FAILS TO NOTICE THE PIT SILENTLY OPENING BEHIND HIM...
NO!
All too easy. Perhaps you are not as strong as the Emperor thought.
AS VADER ACTIVATES THE CARBON-FREEZE PROCESS...
...LUKE USES THE FORCE TO LEAP TO SAFETY.
Impressive...most impressive.

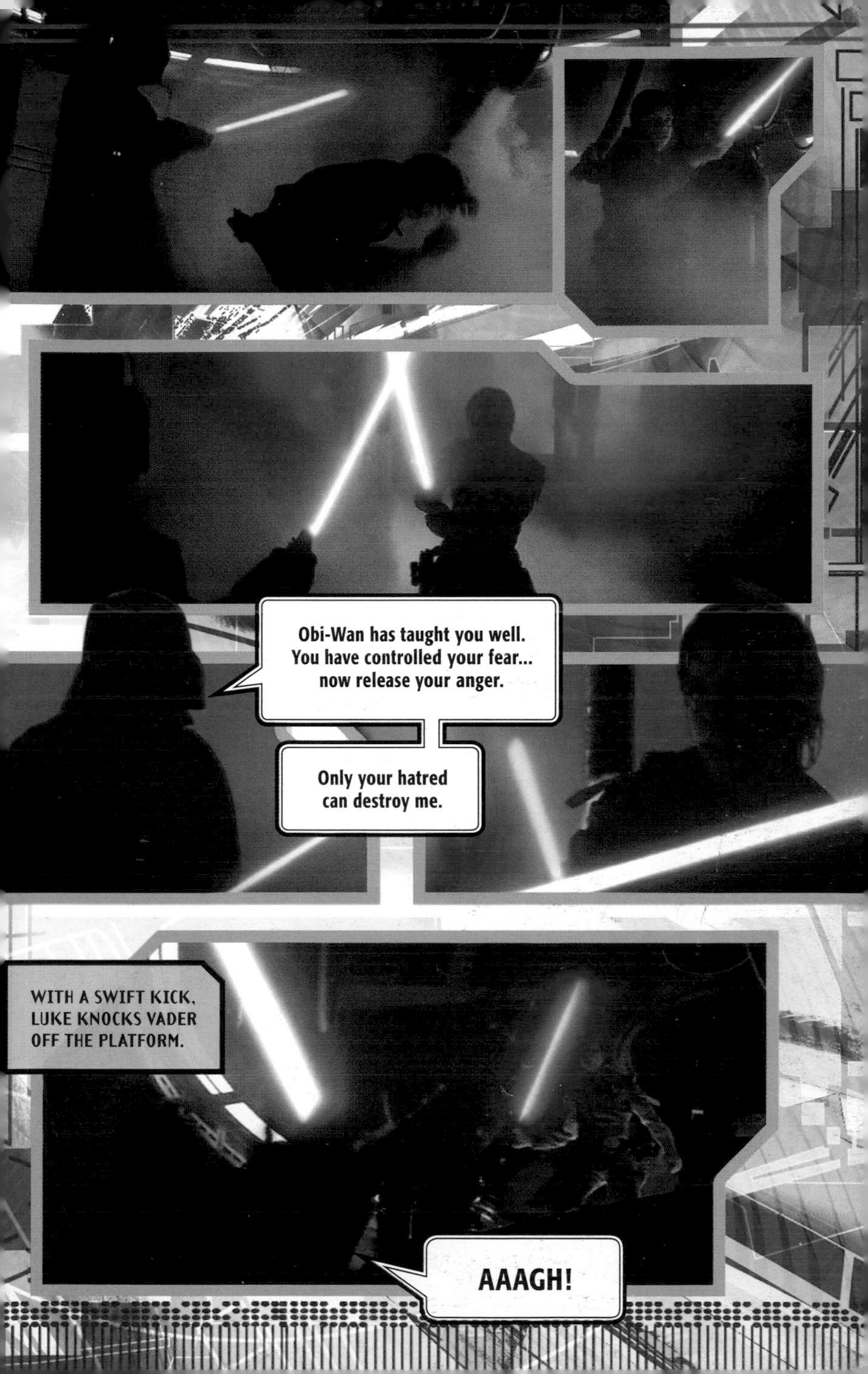
Obi-Wan has taught you well. You have controlled your fear... now release your anger.
Only your hatred can destroy me.
WITH A SWIFT KICK, LUKE KNOCKS VADER OFF THE PLATFORM.
AAAGH!

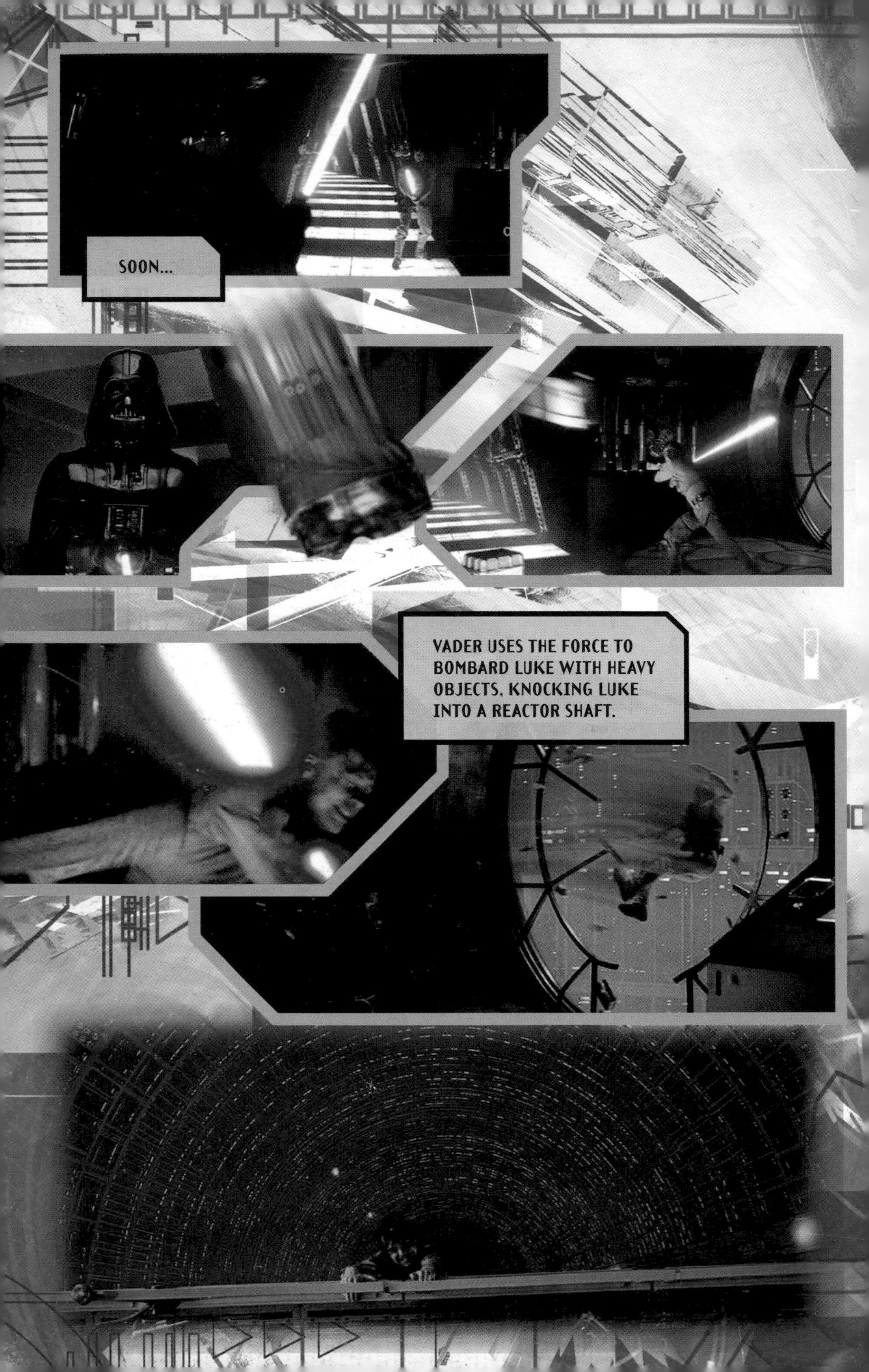
SOON...
VADER USES THE FORCE TO BOMBARD LUKE WITH HEAVY OBJECTS, KNOCKING LUKE INTO A REACTOR SHAFT.

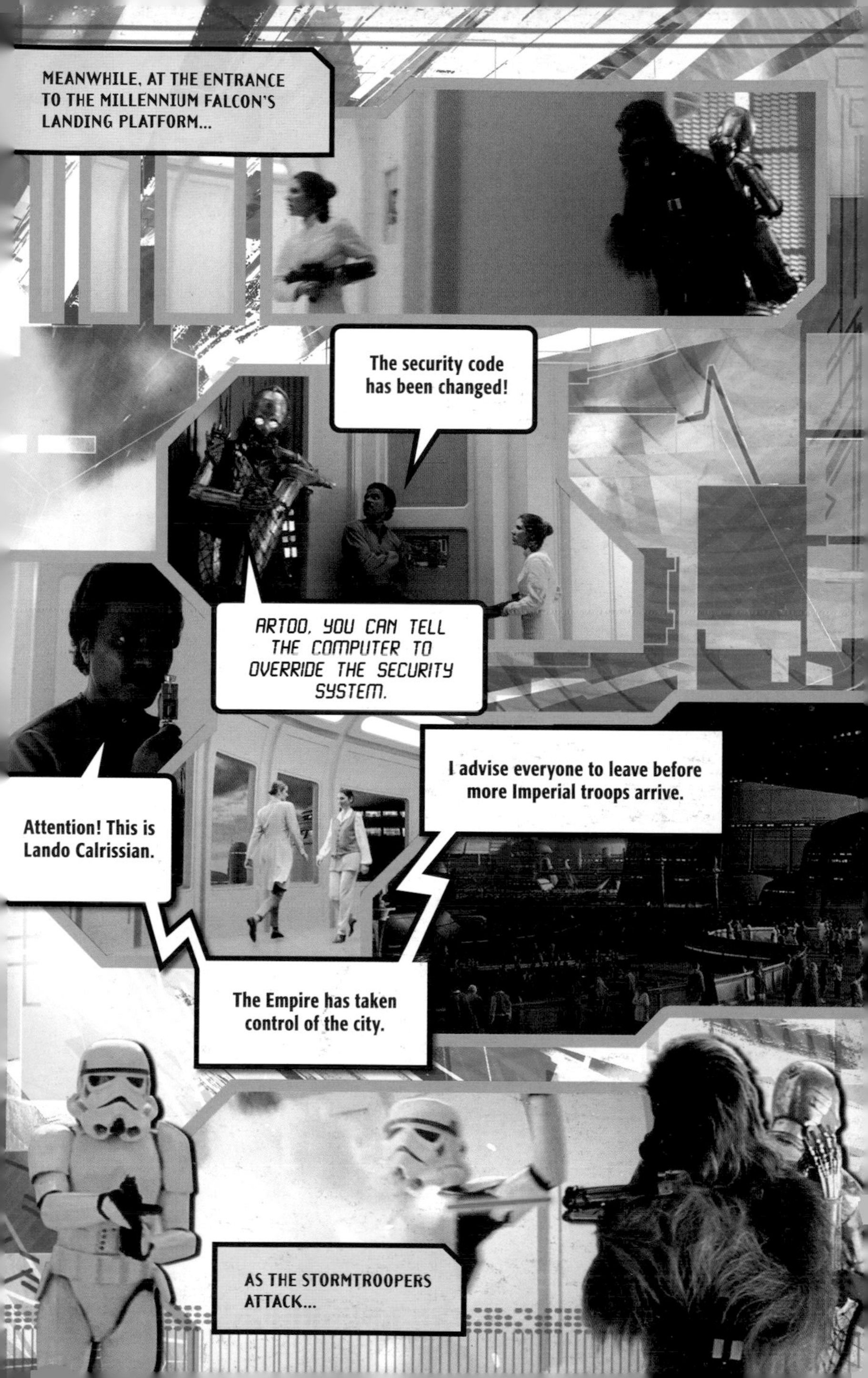
MEANWHILE, AT THE ENTRANCE TO THE MILLENNIUM FALCON'S LANDING PLATFORM...
The security code has been changed!
ARTOO, YOU CAN TELL THE COMPUTER TO OVERRIDE THE SECURITY SYSTEM.
Attention! This is Lando Calrissian.
The Empire has taken control of the city.
I advise everyone to leave before more Imperial troops arrive.
AS THE STORMTROOPERS ATTACK...

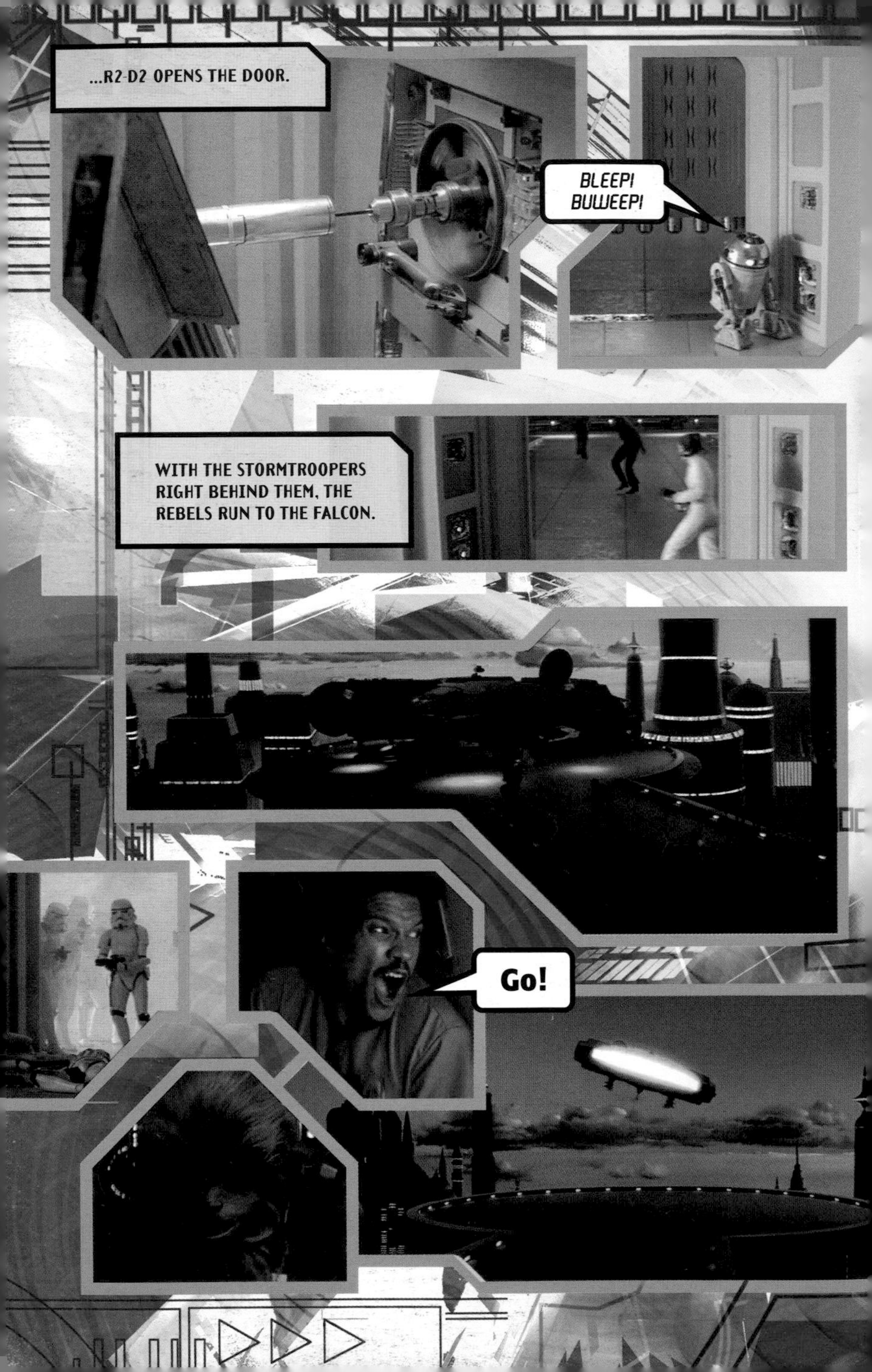
...R2-D2 OPENS THE DOOR.
BLEEP! BUWEEP!
WITH THE STORMTROOPERS RIGHT BEHIND THEM, THE REBELS RUN TO THE FALCON.
Go!

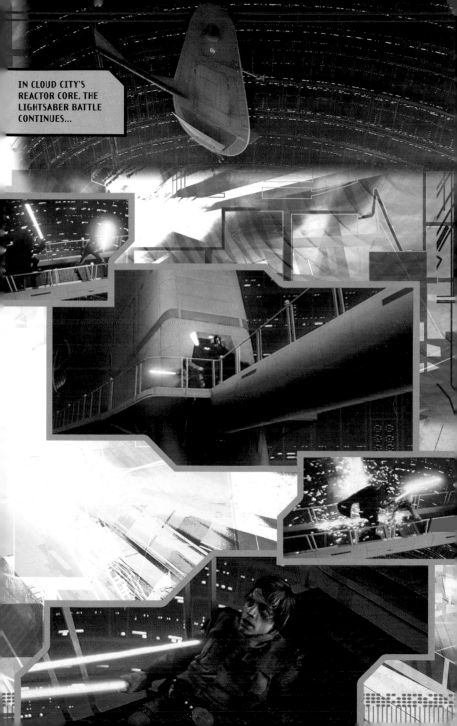

IN CLOUD CITY'S
REACTOR CORE, THE
LIGHTSABER BATTLE
CONTINUES...

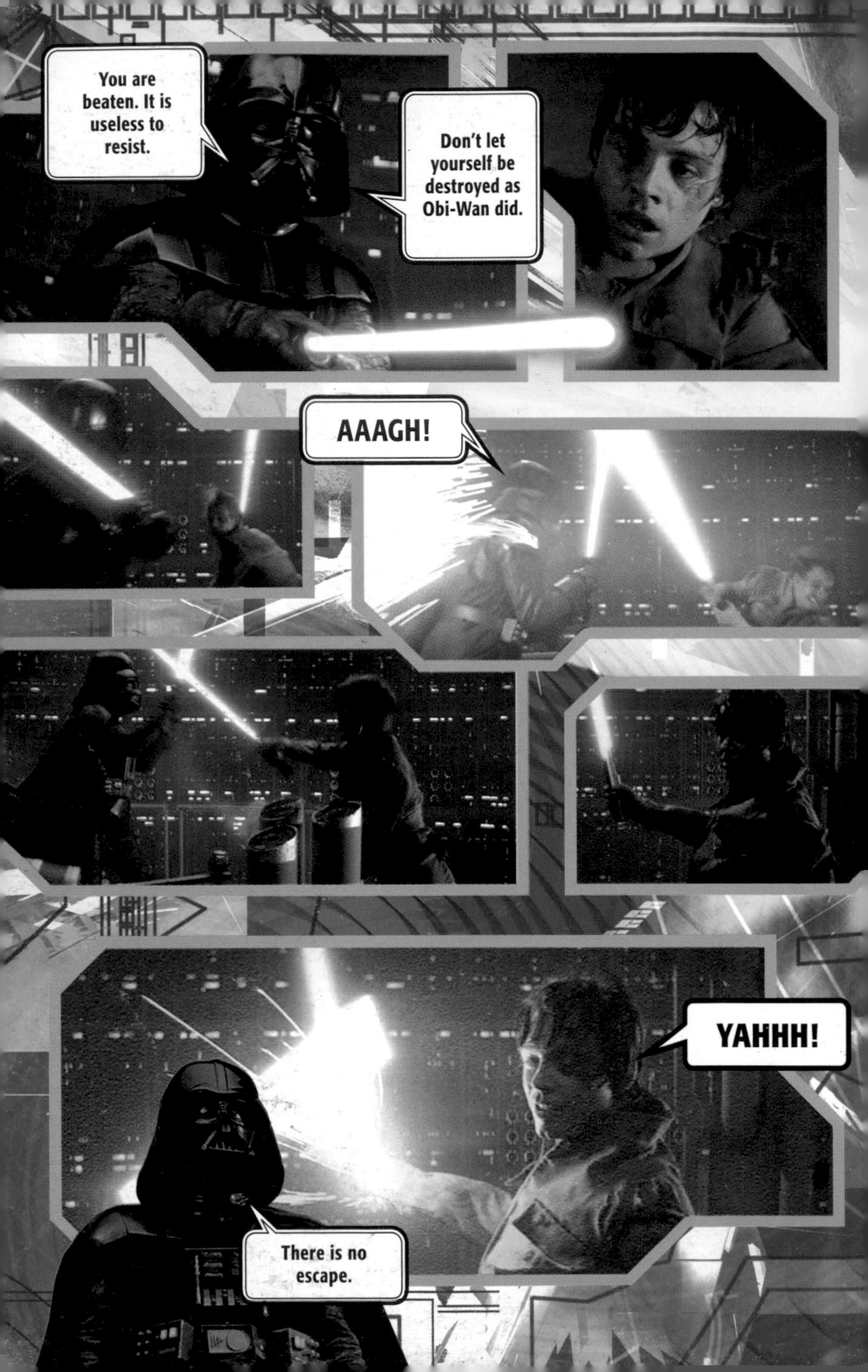
You are beaten. It is useless to resist.
Don't let yourself be destroyed as Obi-Wan did.
AAAGH!
YAHHH!
There is no escape.

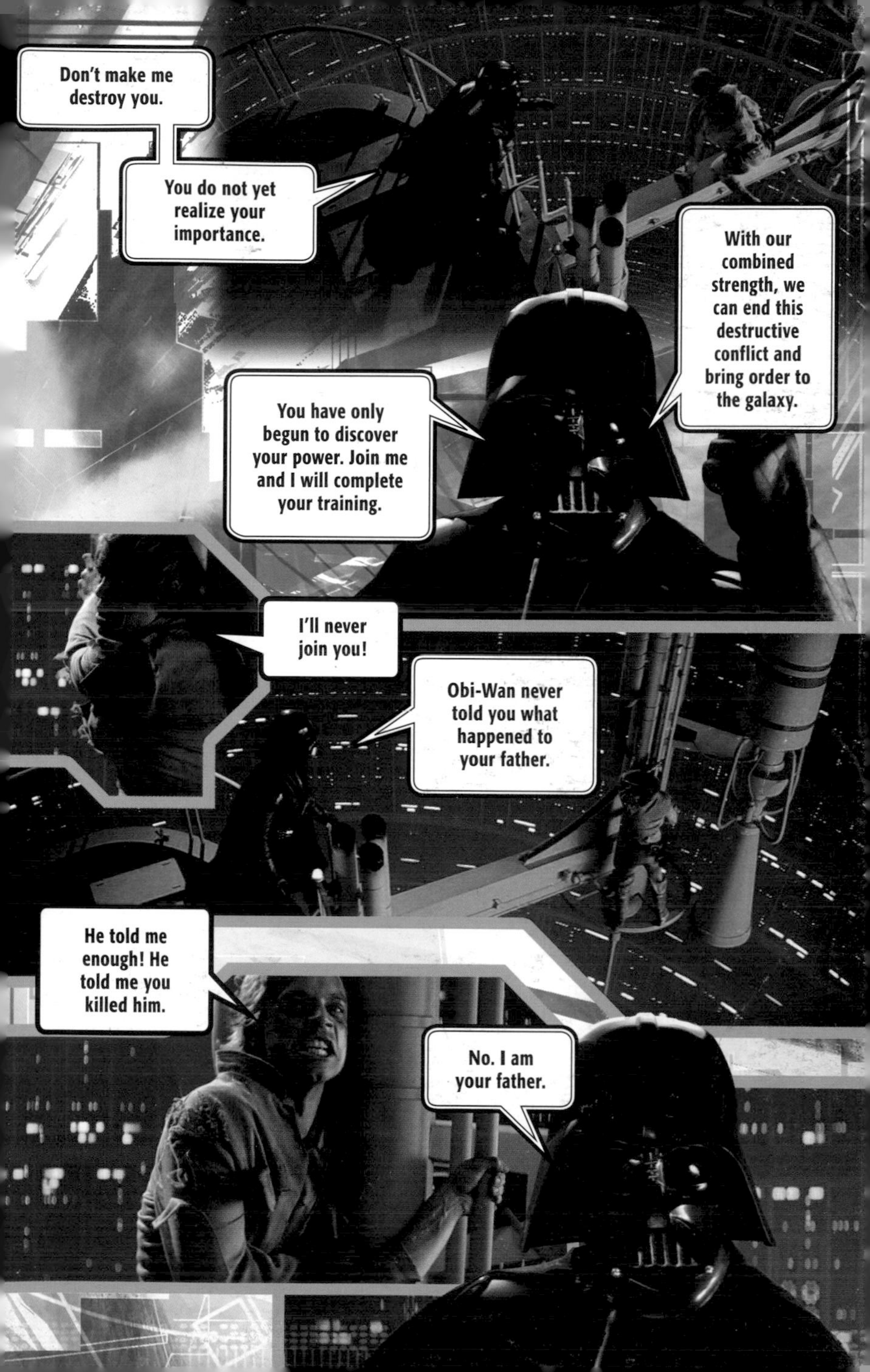
Don't make me destroy you.
You do not yet realize your importance.
You have only begun to discover your power. Join me and I will complete your training.
With our combined strength, we can end this destructive conflict and bring order to the galaxy.
I'll never join you!
Obi-Wan never told you what happened to your father.
He told me enough! He told me you killed him.
No. I am your father.

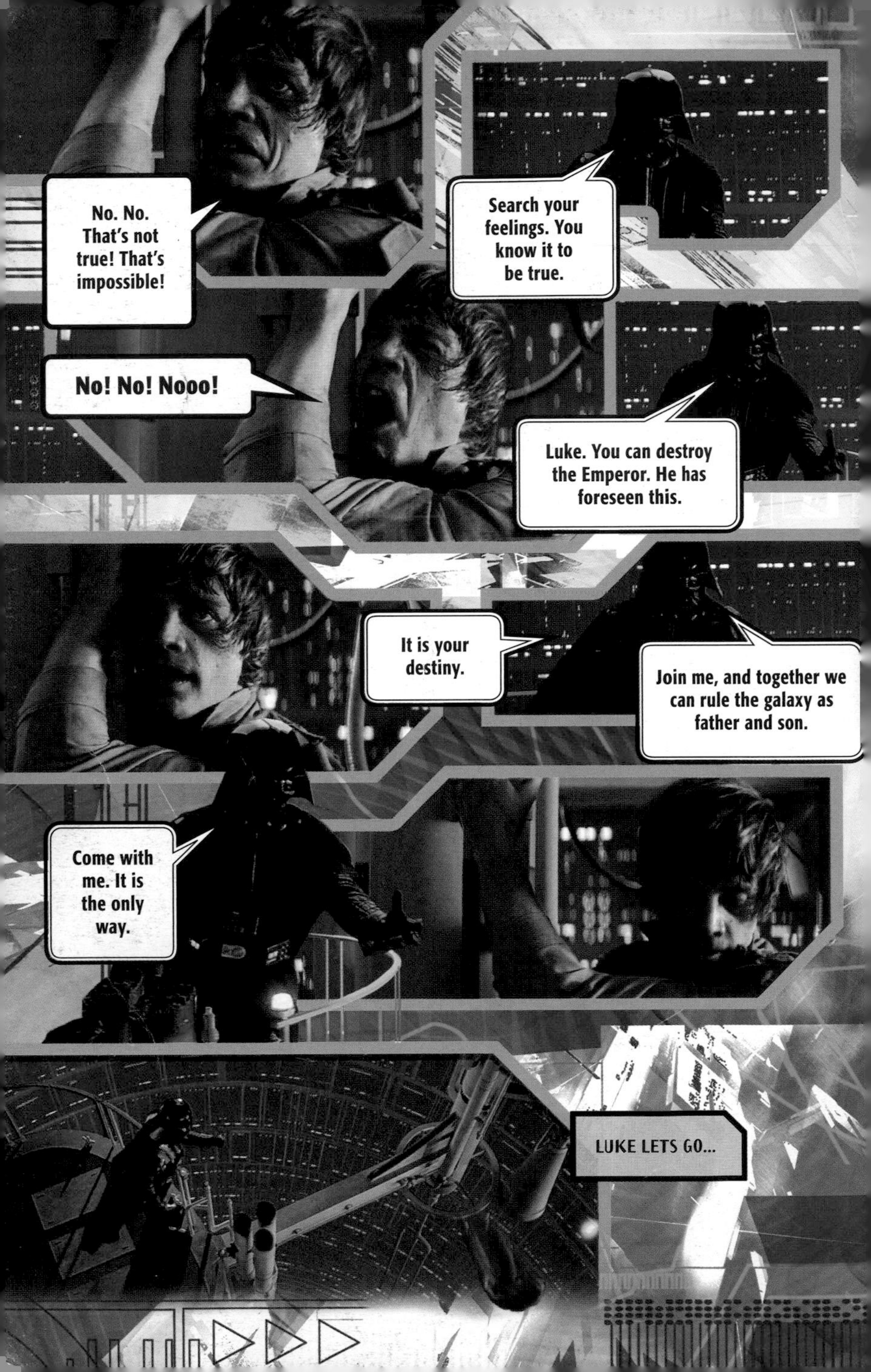
No. No. That's not true! That's impossible!
Search your feelings. You know it to be true.
No! No! Nooo!
Luke. You can destroy the Emperor. He has foreseen this.
It is your destiny.
Join me, and together we can rule the galaxy as father and son.
Come with me. It is the only way.
LUKE LETS GO...

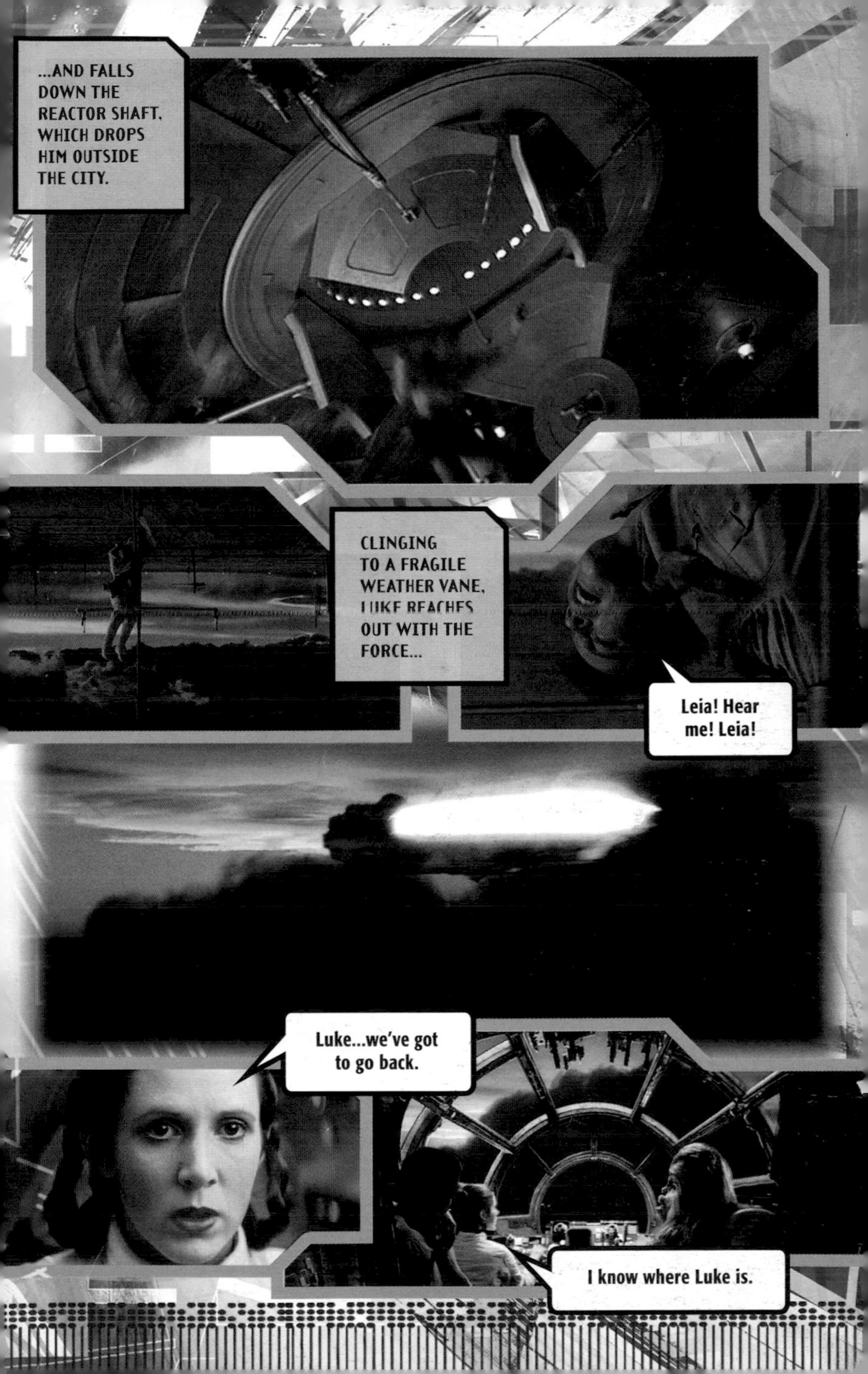
...AND FALLS DOWN THE REACTOR SHAFT, WHICH DROPS HIM OUTSIDE THE CITY.
CLINGING TO A FRAGILE WEATHER VANE, LUKE REACHES OUT WITH THE FORCE...
Leia! Hear me! Leia!
Luke...we've got to go back.
I know where Luke is.

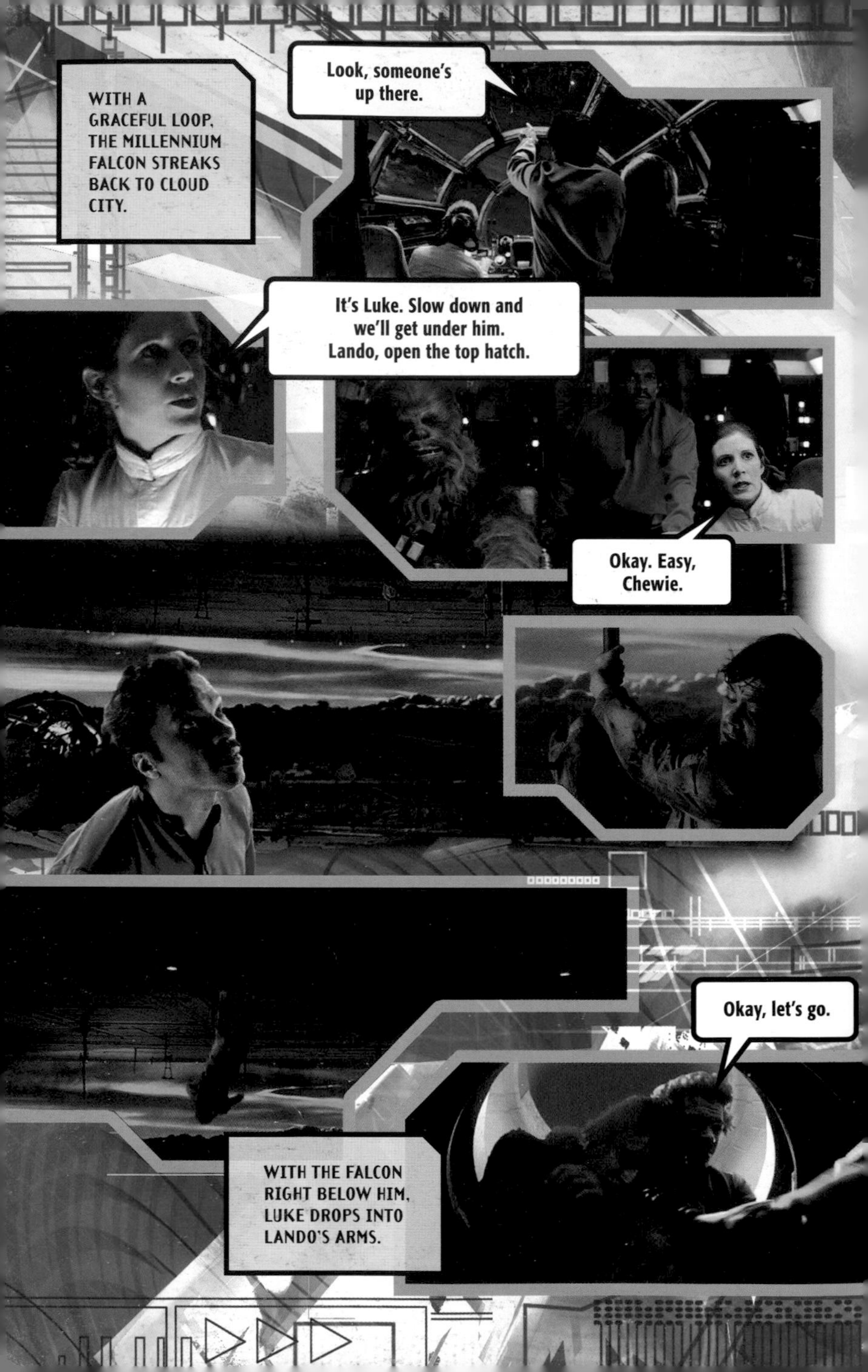
WITH A GRACEFUL LOOP, THE MILLENNIUM FALCON STREAKS BACK TO CLOUD CITY.
Look, someone's up there.
It's Luke. Slow down and we'll get under him. Lando, open the top hatch.
Okay. Easy, Chewie.
Okay, let's go.
WITH THE FALCON RIGHT BELOW HIM, LUKE DROPS INTO LANDO'S ARMS.

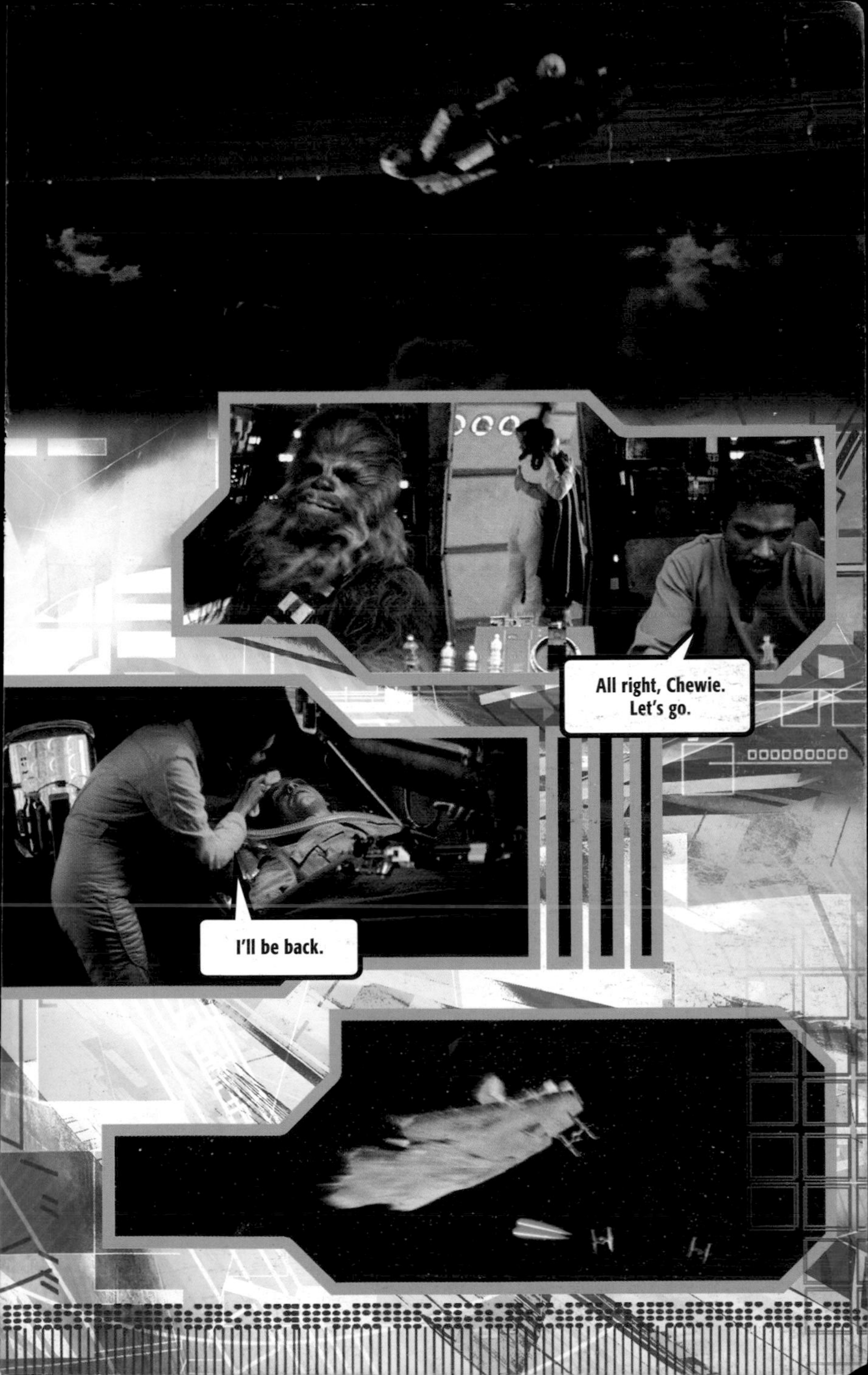
All right, Chewie.
Let's go.
I'll be back.

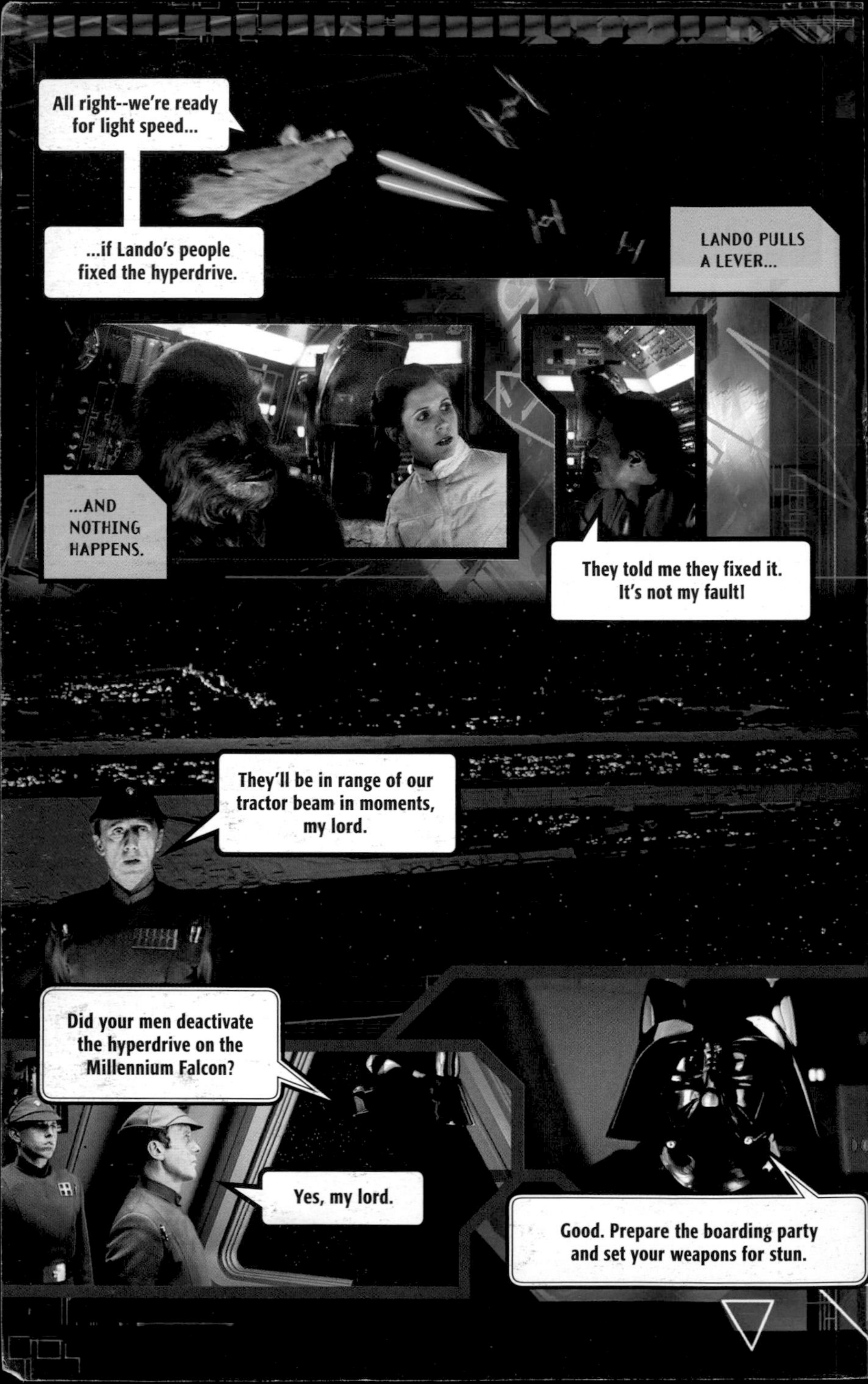
All right--we're ready for light speed...
...if Lando's people fixed the hyperdrive.
LANDO PULLS A LEVER...
...AND NOTHING HAPPENS.
They told me they fixed it. It's not my fault!
They'll be in range of our tractor beam in moments, my lord.
Did your men deactivate the hyperdrive on the Millennium Falcon?
Yes, my lord.
Good. Prepare the boarding party and set your weapons for stun.

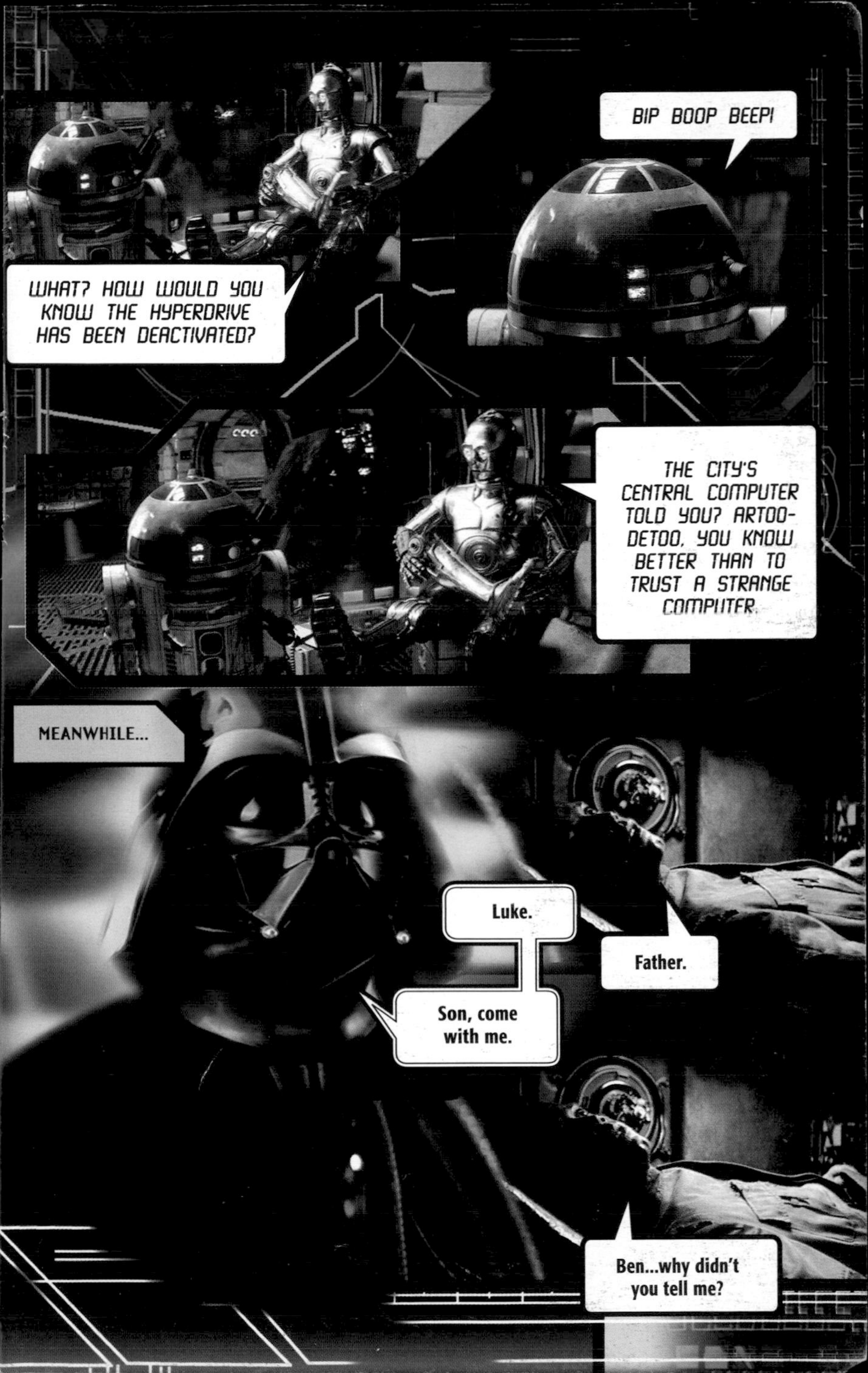
BIP BOOP BEEP!
WHAT? HOW WOULD YOU KNOW THE HYPERDRIVE HAS BEEN DEACTIVATED?
THE CITY'S CENTRAL COMPUTER TOLD YOU? ARTOO-DETOO, YOU KNOW BETTER THAN TO TRUST A STRANGE COMPUTER.
MEANWHILE...
Luke.
Father.
Son, come with me.
Ben...why didn't you tell me?

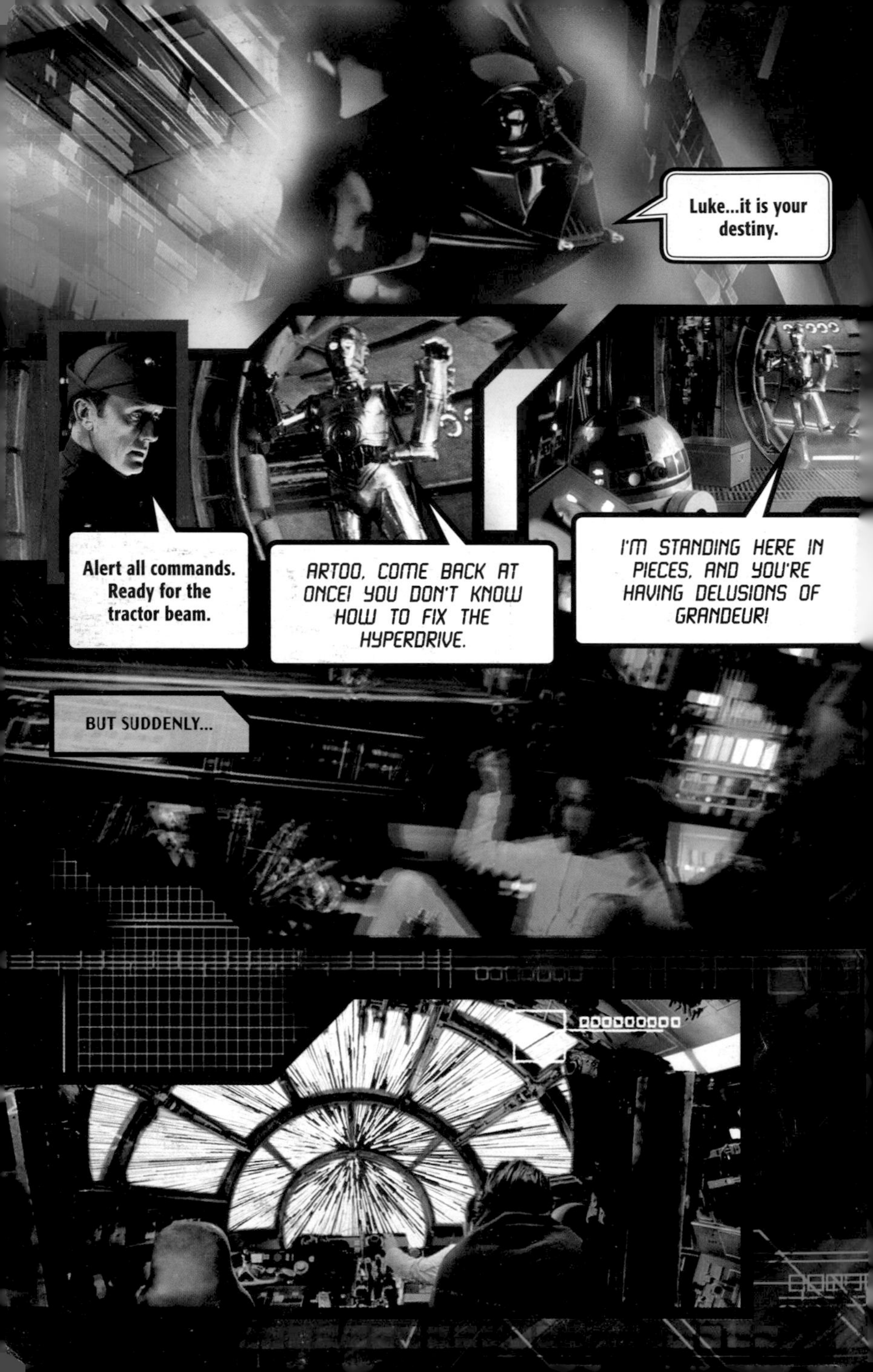
Luke...it is your destiny.
Alert all commands. Ready for the tractor beam.
ARTOO, COME BACK AT ONCE! YOU DON'T KNOW HOW TO FIX THE HYPERDRIVE.
I'M STANDING HERE IN PIECES, AND YOU'RE HAVING DELUSIONS OF GRANDEUR!
BUT SUDDENLY...

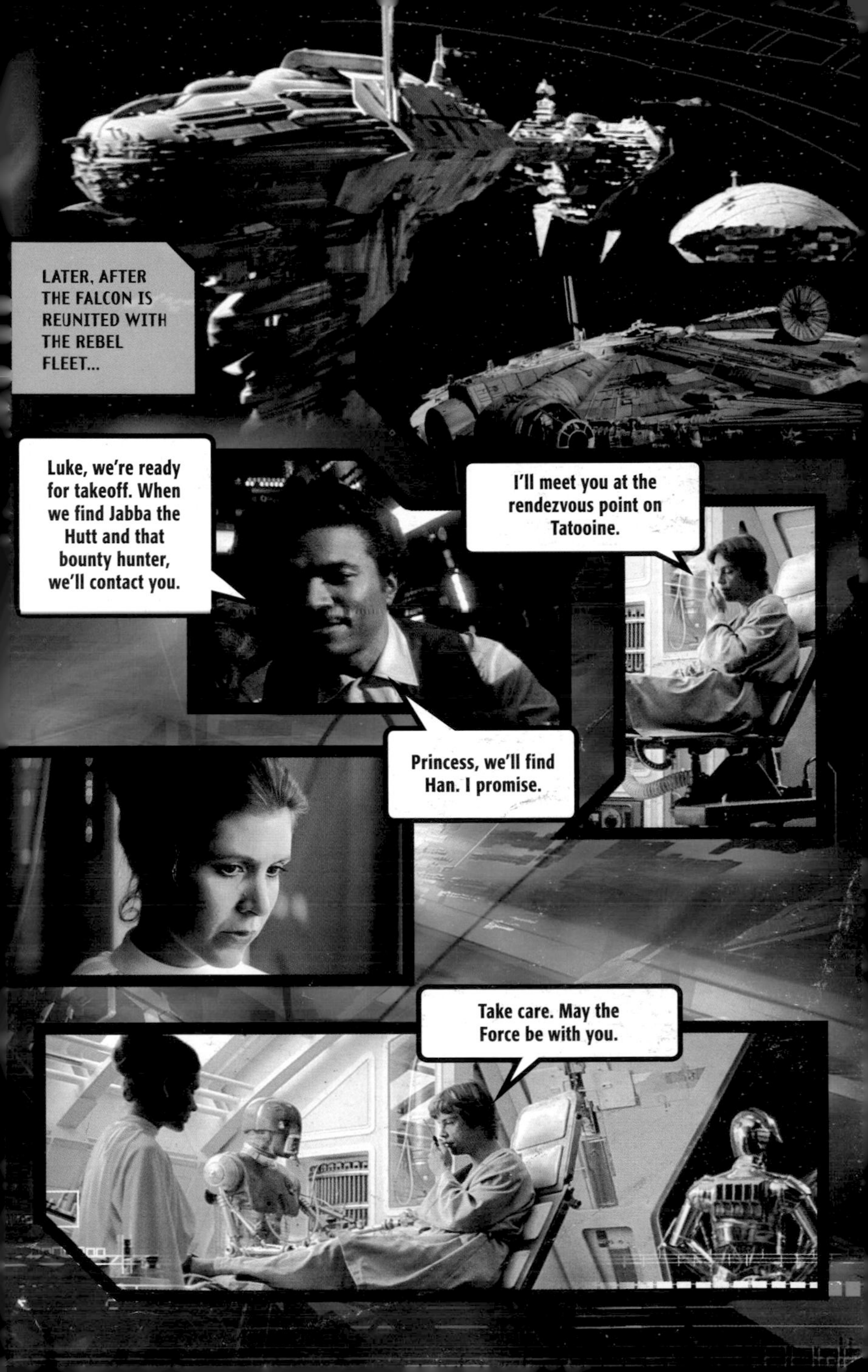
LATER, AFTER THE FALCON IS REUNITED WITH THE REBEL FLEET...
Luke, we're ready for takeoff. When we find Jabba the Hutt and that bounty hunter, we'll contact you.
I'll meet you at the rendezvous point on Tatooine.
Princess, we'll find Han. I promise.
Take care. May the Force be with you.

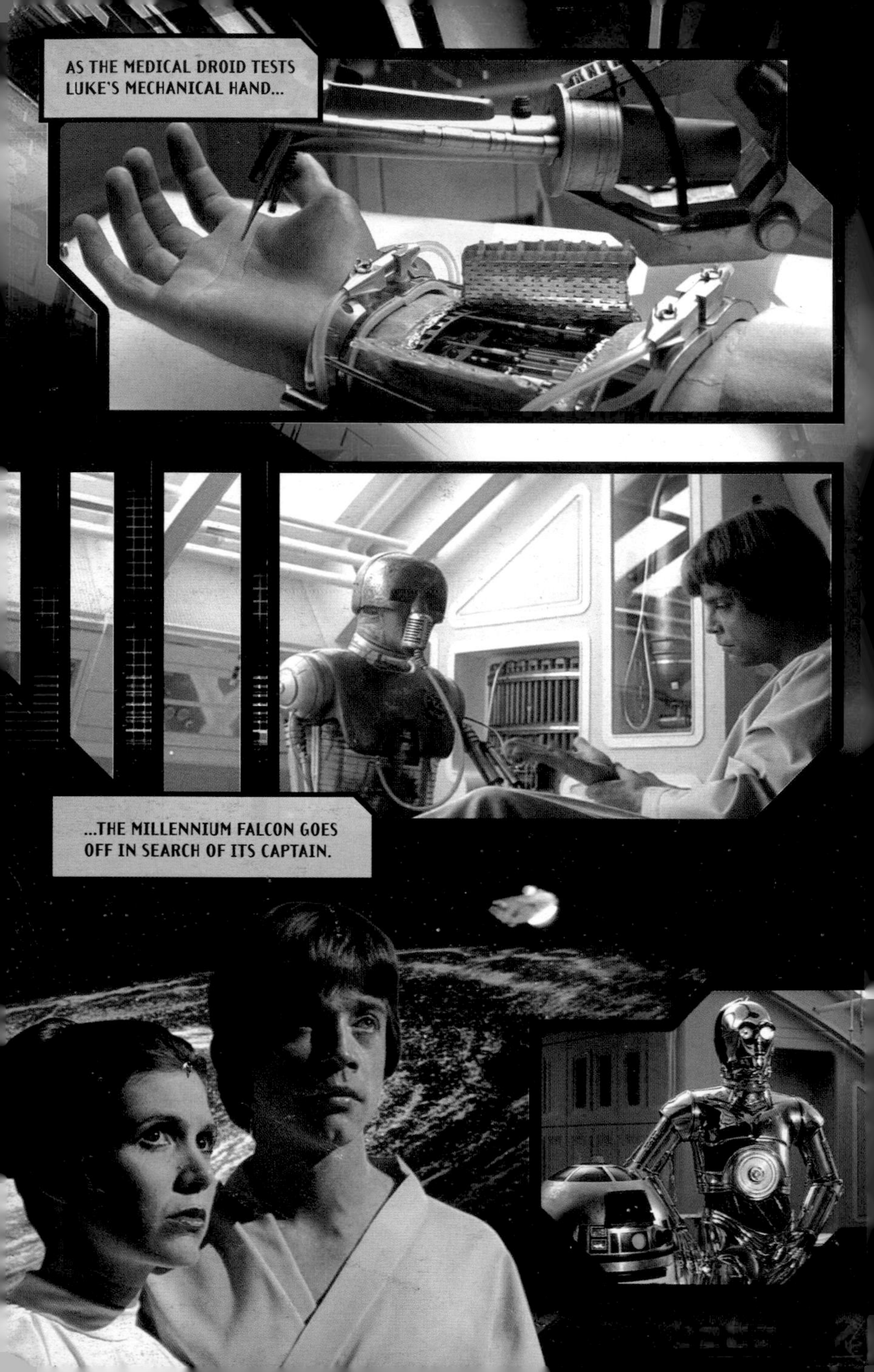
AS THE MEDICAL DROID TESTS LUKE'S MECHANICAL HAND...
...THE MILLENNIUM FALCON GOES OFF IN SEARCH OF ITS CAPTAIN.

DENGAR

Dengar is a grizzled human bounty hunter who hails from Correllia, Han Solo's home planet. His ship is the Punishing One, a Corellian Jumpmaster 5000.

ZUCKUSS

Zuckuss is an insectoid bounty hunter of few words. He is a short, stocky being with a grubby robe, and a number of breather tanks affixed to his head. He hails from the planet Gand and his ship is the Mist Hunter.

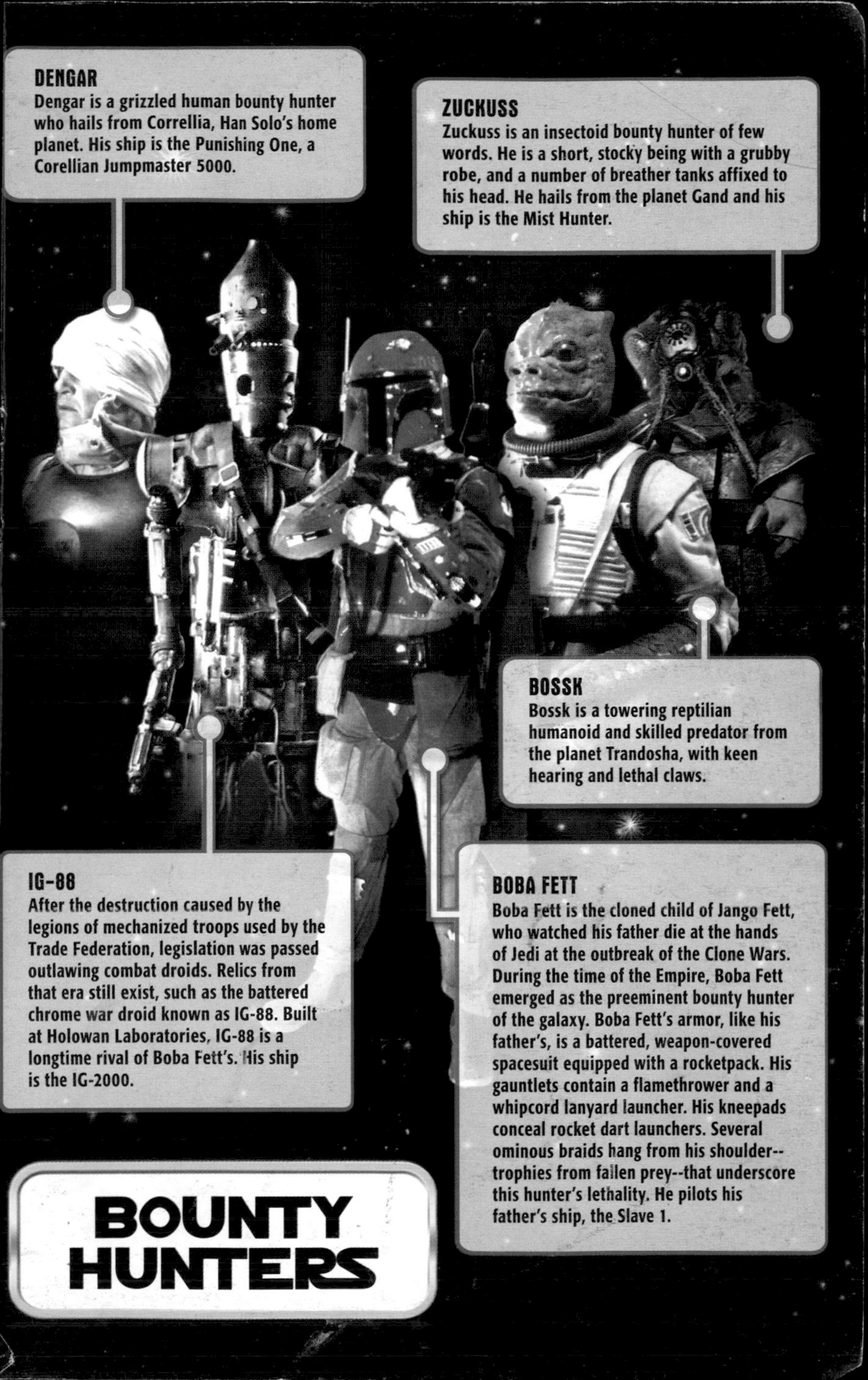

BOSSK

Bossk is a towering reptilian humanoid and skilled predator from the planet Trandosha, with keen hearing and lethal claws.

IG-88

After the destruction caused by the legions of mechanized troops used by the Trade Federation, legislation was passed outlawing combat droids. Relics from that era still exist, such as the battered chrome war droid known as IG-88. Built at Holowan Laboratories, IG-88 is a longtime rival of Boba Fett's. His ship is the IG-2000.

BOBA FETT

Boba Fett is the cloned child of Jango Fett, who watched his father die at the hands of Jedi at the outbreak of the Clone Wars. During the time of the Empire, Boba Fett emerged as the preeminent bounty hunter of the galaxy. Boba Fett's armor, like his father's, is a battered, weapon-covered spacesuit equipped with a rocketpack. His gauntlets contain a flamethrower and a whipcord lanyard launcher. His kneepads conceal rocket dart launchers. Several ominous braids hang from his shoulder--trophies from fallen prey--that underscore this hunter's lethality. He pilots his father's ship, the Slave 1.

BOUNTY HUNTERS

CREATURES AND ALIENS

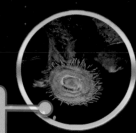

MYNOCK
Leathery-winged manta-like flyers, mynocks are a common pest faced by space travelers. The parasitic creatures attach themselves to hosts via their bristly suction cup-like mouth. Pilots need to examine their ships for mynock infestations, as the creatures like to affix to starships and chew on their power cables. Mynocks travel in packs and typically grow to be 1.6 meters long with a wingspan of approximately 1.25 meters.

SPACE SLUG
Space slugs are colossal, worm-like creatures that reside within the furrows and craters of asteroids and airless planetoids. The slug's bizarre biology allows it to survive in the vacuum of space. Space slugs have been seen to grow up to 800 meters in length. The chaotic Hoth asteroid field is known to host such a massive specimen.

WAMPA
The bone-chilling cold is not the only danger that awaits a traveler on the Hoth plains. Despite standing over two meters in height, the wampa ice creature is nonetheless a stealthy predator. Its white fur is the perfect camouflage, and the howling Hoth winds mask its approach until it is too late. With a crushing blow from its clawed hand, a wampa is strong enough to snap the neck of even a hardy tauntaun.

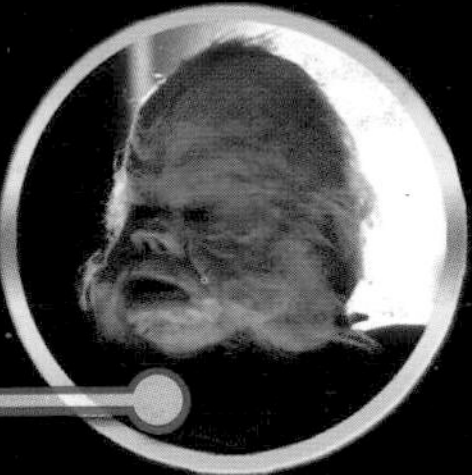

UGNAUGHT

Ugnaughts are a species of humanoid-porcine beings who live and work on Bespin's Cloud City. They are usually found in the Tibanna gas processing plants or as general laborers throughout the city. Ugnaught workers are barely one meter tall, have pink skin, hog-like snouts and teeth, and long hair. Their clothes are gray, with blue smocks.

TAUNTAUN

Tauntauns are a species of snow lizard found roaming the windswept snow plains of Hoth. The Rebel Alliance domesticated the swift creature during their stay on the ice planet and used the animals for patrol duties outside Echo Base. The animals proved useful, as the Rebel technicians had difficulty adapting their repulsorlift speeders to the subzero temperatures. As Han Solo noted, they smell bad on the outside and even worse on the inside.

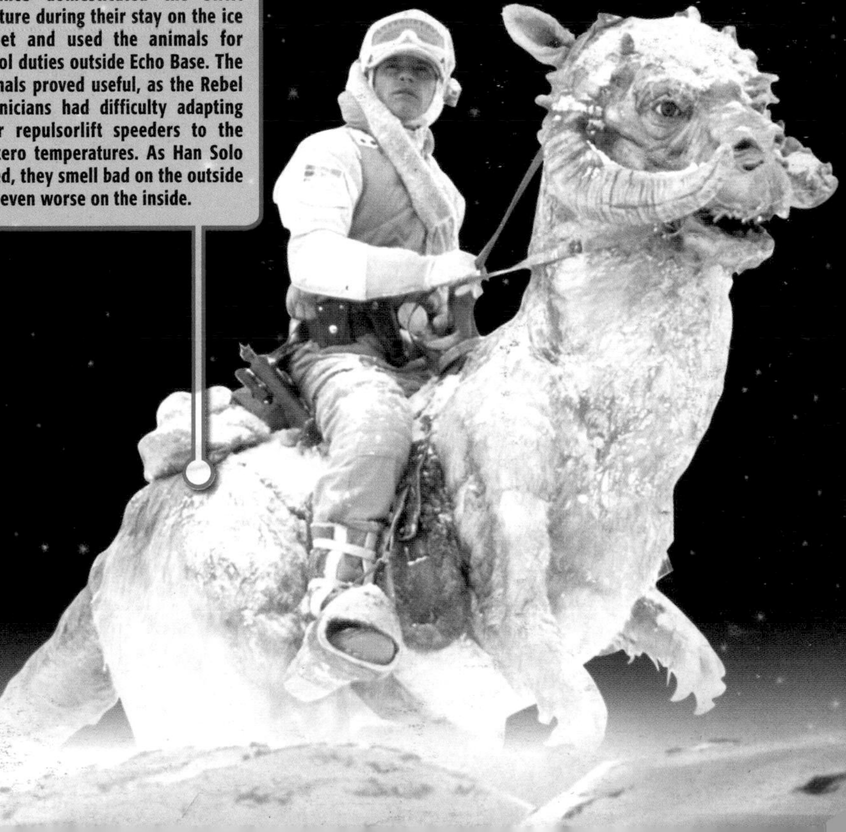

STAR WARS GRAPHIC NOVEL TIMELINE (IN YEARS

Tales of the Jedi—5,000–3,986 BSW4
Knights of the Old Republic—3,964 BSW4
Jedi vs. Sith—1,000 BSW4
Jedi Council: Acts of War—33 BSW4
Prelude to Rebellion—33 BSW4
Darth Maul—33 BSW4
Episode I: The Phantom Menace—32 BSW4
Outlander—32 BSW4
Emissaries to Malastare—32 BSW4
Jango Fett: Open Seasons—32 BSW4
Twilight—31 BSW4
Bounty Hunters—31 BSW4
The Hunt for Aurra Sing—30 BSW4
Darkness—30 BSW4
The Stark Hyperspace War—30 BSW4
Rite of Passage—28 BSW4
Jango Fett—27 BSW4
Zam Wesell—27 BSW4
Honor and Duty—24 BSW4
Episode II: Attack of the Clones—22 BSW4
Clone Wars—22–19 BSW4
Clone Wars Adventures—22–19 BSW4
General Grievous—20 BSW4
Episode III: Revenge of the Sith—19 BSW4
Dark Times—19 BSW4
Droids—3 BSW4
Boba Fett: Enemy of the Empire—2 BSW4
Underworld—1 BSW4
Episode IV: A New Hope—SW4
Classic Star Wars—0–3 ASW4
A Long Time Ago . . .—0–4 ASW4
Empire—0 ASW4
Rebellion—0 ASW4
Vader's Quest—0 ASW4
Boba Fett: Man with a Mission—0 ASW4
Jabba the Hutt: The Art of the Deal—1 ASW4
Splinter of the Mind's Eye—1 ASW4
Episode V: The Empire Strikes Back—3 ASW4
Shadows of the Empire—3–5 ASW4
Episode VI: Return of the Jedi—4 ASW4
X-Wing Rogue Squadron—4–5 ASW4
Mara Jade: By the Emperor's Hand—4 ASW4
Heir to the Empire—9 ASW4
Dark Force Rising—9 ASW4
The Last Command—9 ASW4
Dark Empire—10 ASW4
Boba Fett: Death, Lies, and Treachery—11 ASW4
Crimson Empire—11 ASW4
Jedi Academy: Leviathan—13 ASW4
Union—20 ASW4
Chewbacca—25 ASW4
Legacy—130 ASW4

Old Republic Era
25,000 – 1000 years before
Star Wars: A New Hope

Rise of the Empire Era
1000 – 0 years before
Star Wars: A New Hope

Rebellion Era
0 – 5 years after
Star Wars: A New Hope

New Republic Era
5 – 25 years after
Star Wars: A New Hope

New Jedi Order Era
25+ years after
Star Wars: A New Hope

Legacy Era
130+ years after
Star Wars: A New Hope

Infinities
Does not apply to timeline

Sergio Aragonés Stomps Star Wars
Star Wars Tales
Star Wars Infinities
Tag and Bink
Star Wars Visionaries

BSW4 = before *Episode IV: A New Hope*. ASW4 = after *Episode IV: A New Hope*.